Leading
Effective
Secondary
School Reform

Mikie would like to dedicate this book to her husband, parents, and family, who have supported and encouraged her career as a high school administrator and, most recently, as an author; and a special dedication "to my two guardian angel mentors, the late Dr. John Stallings and Raymond Monti . . . for their guidance and profound influence, and who taught me everything I know."

Loren dedicates this book to Frank and Joey, her parents, family, friends, and mentors who have "guided and supported me in my educational leadership quest. There has never been a dull moment!"

Leading
Effective
Secondary
School Reform

Your Guide to
Strategies That Work

Mikie Longridge   Loren R. Tarantino

CORWIN PRESS
A Sage Publications Company
Thousand Oaks, California

For information:

Corwin Press
A Sage Publications Company
2455 Teller Road
Thousand Oaks, California 91320
www.corwinpress.com

Sage Publications Ltd
1 Oliver's Yard
55 City Road
London EC1Y 1SP
United Kingdom

Sage Publications India Pvt. Ltd.
B-42, Panchsheel Enclave
Post Box 4109
New Delhi 110 017 India

Printed in the United States of America

Library of Congress Cataloging-in-Publication Data

Loughridge, Mikie.
Leading effective secondary school reform : your guide to strategies that work / Mikie Loughridge and Loren R. Tarantino.
        p. cm.
Includes bibliographical references and index.
ISBN 1-4129-0604-0 (cloth) — ISBN 1-4129-0605-9 (pbk.)
    1. School improvement programs—United States—Case studies. 2. Middle schools—United States—Administration—Case studies. 3. High schools—United States—Administration—Case studies. 4. Educational leadership—United States—Case studies. I. Tarantino, Loren R. II. Title.
LB2822.82.L68 2005
373.12—dc22

                                                            2004016458

This book is printed on acid-free paper.

04   05   06   07   08   09   10   9   8   7   6   5   4   3   2   1

Acquisitions Editor:	Elizabeth Brenkus
Production Editor:	Kristen Gibson
Copy Editor:	Teresa Herlinger
Typesetter:	C&M Digitals (P) Ltd.
Indexer:	Rick Hurd
Cover Designer:	Michael Dubowe

Contents

List of Figures

Preface

School leaders maneuver within very complex and defined systems that converge on the ultimate objective of improving student achievement. They influence the efforts of the learning community to improve student achievement through the beliefs, skills, and experiences they bring to the position.

What would happen if a site administrator led without a clear vision or an understanding of the school and district mission? Can the change process be ignored? How much sharing or delegating must occur for a culture of shared leadership to exist? Can student achievement improve without teachers using student work to inform curriculum and instruction? Can teachers improve their practice without a coherent professional development plan? Most important, what is the role of site administrators in creating successful learning communities?

No effective leader, especially at a secondary school, can hope to monitor all of the complex priorities and initiatives alone. Nonetheless, the school leader will be held accountable for their success or failure, and ultimately, for student performance.

Common Beliefs

In developing the premise for this book, the authors have incorporated the following common beliefs about managing complex change in secondary schools:

- Schools must have a clear vision of what student performance will look like in the future.
- A successful learning community acknowledges that change is a process, not an event, and that it takes time and buy-in from all stakeholders.

- Change is intimidating and challenges comfort zones. Yet change is inevitable if success is to be realized.
- Effective leaders empower others to provide leadership within the learning community.

Leading Effective Secondary School Reform: Your Guide to Strategies That Work not only sets the stage for school leaders embarking on a new assignment or facing a new set of mandates, it also provides activities, agendas, and tips for successful planning and implementation around improving the achievement of all students. Strategies outlined in this book will empower secondary school leaders to successfully maneuver through the change process, provide needed and appropriate support to all stakeholders, and develop a comprehensive Single School Plan with an aligned professional development component within a professional learning community. The book presents a concise, easy-to-use guide for school leaders at secondary schools.

A myriad of books exist about leadership for school administrators facing complex changes in their schools. This book will focus on three variables that influence critical attributes of successful leadership at secondary schools. Variables are influenced by a leader's beliefs, skills, and experiences. The three variables presented in this book will provide a focal point for the three main sections of the book. These variables are (1) Vision, (2) Shared Decision Making, and (3) Assessment and Accountability.

Critical attributes are ingredients of effective school leadership that align with the identified variable. Each chapter highlights a critical attribute for leading effective secondary school reform. Eight critical attributes are covered in the first eight chapters of this book:

Part I: Vision

    Chapter 1: School Culture

    Chapter 2: The Change Process

    Chapter 3: The Single School Plan

Part II: Shared Decision Making

    Chapter 4: Professional Development

    Chapter 5: Professional Learning Communities

    Chapter 6: Parent Involvement

Part III: Assessment and Accountability

　　Chapter 7: Action Research

　　Chapter 8: Productive Classroom Observations

　　Chapter 9: Putting the Pieces Together

The last chapter synthesizes the strategies in the previous eight chapters into a checklist for getting started in the school reform process. Using a *case-study format*, this book will consider the actions made by four secondary school leaders as they wrestle with the challenges of implementing state and federal mandates. Each chapter will present a set of case study scenarios to describe how the principals' decisions about a critical attribute of leadership influenced their learning communities. *Points to consider* follow the case study scenarios. *Application activities* are also included, to allow school leaders to reflect on their own school environment and culture through the lens of each chapter.

Case Studies

The case study schools and leaders in this book represent a synthesis of characteristics from large and medium-size schools in urban and suburban areas. It should be noted that these case studies are based on real people and situations at schools across the nation. They are not figments of the authors' imagination. However, names have been changed to protect the innocent! All four schools are involved in an "underperforming" school program. Site administrators featured in this book are from two middle schools and two high schools. They represent various leadership styles that characterize their decision-making and problem-solving strategies. Mary M. and Tony R. represent middle school principals; Carl A. and Anna S. represent high school principals. All four are relatively new principals with zero to two years of experience. As you read the case studies and suggested strategies, you may recognize actions you have taken as a school leader.

Case Study Middle School Leaders

 Mary M. is the principal at Greenview Middle School. She is beginning her first year as a principal. Her leadership experience has been primarily as a co-administrator at Greenview Middle School for three years. She is known as a decisive, highly structured, and directive administrator. She is very task oriented and is motivated to complete assigned tasks.

RVMS Tony R. is the principal at Ridge View Middle School. He has completed his second year at the school. Prior to becoming a principal, Tony was a co-administrator for five years. He has worked on the district strategic-planning team and has been active in the district office staff-development program for the past three years. He is known as an organized, relationship-oriented administrator.

Middle School Demographics

Each middle school has approximately 1200 seventh- and eighth-grade students and has a principal and two co-administrators. Both schools are in their third year as designated "program improvement," based on Adequate Yearly Progress (AYP) factors. The student population is made up of 40 percent white, 35 percent Hispanic, 10 percent Asian, 10 percent African American, and 5 percent other ethnic representation. Ten percent of the students are enrolled in special education classes and 35 percent of the students are designated Limited English Proficient. Both schools are designated schoolwide Title I schools. Each school is located in an urban, low socioeconomic neighborhood. Both schools were built approximately 10 years ago.

Case Study: High School Leaders

MHS Anna S. is beginning her second year as the principal at Municipal High School. Prior to her current assignment, she was a co-administrator at a middle school and a high school. Over the past four years, Anna has been an active member and leader of several district committees in curriculum and instruction, including literacy, textbook selection, and student assessment. She is known as a student advocate and an academically oriented administrator.

BKHS Carl A. is a first-year principal at Birch Knoll High School. He has been a co-administrator for six years, the past three years at Birch Knoll High School. Carl has participated in numerous school projects such as selection of library resource material, Back-to-School night, developing a school discipline plan, and identifying school-community partnerships. Carl is known as a team player, delegator, and relationship-oriented administrator. Completing assigned tasks motivates Carl.

Each high school has approximately 2500 ninth- through twelfth-grade students and has a principal and three co-administrators. Both schools are in their third year as designated "underperforming schools," based on AYP factors. The student population is made up of 48 percent African American, 27 percent Hispanic, 20 percent white, and 5 percent other ethnic representation. Twenty-five percent of the students are enrolled in special education classes and 15 percent of the students are designated Limited English Proficient. Both schools are designated schoolwide Title I schools. Each school is located in a suburban, medium socioeconomic neighborhood. Both schools were built approximately 70 years ago and are considered the "flagship" schools for their districts.

Secondary School Challenges

The authors believe that secondary schools present unique challenges for site administrators. The culture of secondary schools tends to be very different from that of elementary schools, with a whole different set of beliefs, values, norms, and attitudes. Secondary schools tend to be bigger, have more student activities, be departmentalized, and be more competitive in relation to other schools in the district. Secondary schools often have minimal parent involvement and are dealing with students in the throes of "hormone hell." As a result of these unique challenges, we feel that it is important to view these schools from the secondary perspective, to allow school leaders to consider viable solutions as they manage complex change in leading effective secondary school reform.

Authors' Note

This book does not address safety and security issues. The authors, however, recognize that it is extremely difficult to focus on an academic reform agenda if major safety concerns at the school are unresolved. Effective school leaders must ensure that these issues are continuously addressed to allow instructional reforms to move forward.

We hope that school leaders reading this book will recognize behaviors and decisions in the case studies and be open to considering some of the tips, strategies, and techniques outlined in the chapters.

Finally, like all good references, *Leading Effective Secondary School Reform: Your Guide to Strategies That Work* is intended to spark your creativity and ignite your resolve to develop strategies and solutions for your own environment.

As the English poet Samuel Butler once said, *"Life is like playing the violin solo in public and learning the instrument as one goes on."*

Acknowledgments

We are grateful to the people at Corwin Press, especially Cyndee Callan, Faye Zucker, Stacy Wagner, Robb Clouse, and Lizzie Brenkus, for holding our hands and drying our tears throughout the creation and development of this book—especially the title. A special thank you to Teresa Herlinger, for her invaluable assistance with the final edits. We are also indebted to Frank Tarantino, Katie Satterfield, Karen Janney, Dr. Barbara Walkington, Diane Alexander, Dr. Sylvia Ibarra, Cathy Hicks, Rabbi Michoel Peikes, and the Southwest and Palm Springs' Girls for their suggestions, edits, coaching, encouragement, and overall moral support.

Corwin Press gratefully acknowledges the contributions of the following individuals:

Russ Bennett
Principal
Harmon Middle School
Aurora, OH

Lexy Conte
Principal
Amargosa Creek Middle School
Lancaster, CA

Russell Dever
Superintendent
Mainland Regional High School
Linwood, NJ

Todd Edwards
Assistant Professor
Dept. of Education &
    Allied Studies

John Carol University
University Heights, OH

G. Steven Griggs
Author, Principal
Francis Howell Central
    High School
St. Charles, MO

John Hannum
Superintendent
High Point Regional
    School District
Sussex, NJ

Karen Janney
ACSA 2004 Principal
    of the Year
Montgomery High School
San Diego, CA

Frank Kawtoski
Retired Principal ('04)
Director of Secondary
   Education
Morrisville School District
Morrisville, PA

Lawrence L. Marazza
Author

Lighthouse
   Management Group
Russell, OH

J. Victor McGuire
Instructor
College of Education
University of Nevada
Las Vegas, NV

About the Authors

Mikie Loughridge is currently serving as a secondary Principal Coach for the Los Angeles County Office of Education and the Southern California Comprehensive Assistance Center's Office of the Regional System of District and School Support (RSDSS). She served as a special education teacher at the middle and high school levels, as a continuation high school teacher, and as a high school vice principal and principal. Her district office experience includes holding the position of Director of Curriculum and Instruction and Director of Teacher Support and Employee Development for the Antelope Valley Union High School District, as well as an Induction Consultant for the California Commission on Teacher Credentialing and the California Department of Education. She served as adjunct faculty for eighteen years in teacher and administrative preparation programs at four private and state universities. She also developed and presented a variety of workshops at the local, regional, state, and national levels. She holds a doctorate in Organizational Leadership from the University of Southern California.

Loren R. Tarantino has a unique history of employment and training in education. Loren has 30 years in education. She has been the principal of a private high school in San Diego, California, and has worked in public schools as a secondary school classroom teacher, middle school administrator, and district office administrator in student support services, curriculum and instruction, and human resources. In addition, Loren was a consultant with the California Attorney General's School/Law Enforcement Partnership Cadre, the California Commission on Teacher Credentialing, and the California Department of Education. Since 1986, she has presented local, state and national conference keynote speeches and workshops for school board, teacher, and school administrator associations and universities on a variety of topics including beginning teacher induction, conflict resolution, communication strategies, and conducting classroom observations.

PART I

Vision

1

School Culture

How We Do Things Around Here

How often has this happened? A new or existing principal is faced with moving his or her school through some major reform effort and puts together an ambitious plan to get *it* done, complete with goals, objectives, timelines, and designated responsibilities. The plan has been presented to the staff, who has responded cautiously, not at all, or negatively. The administrator begins to move the process forward and runs into the proverbial brick wall. The school is going through the motions of change, but in reality, nothing is really changing in the way the school does business.

Two scenarios play themselves out over and over again in secondary schools engaged in the reform process. Both scenarios involve the hidden attribute "school culture." One scenario involves a new principal or co-administrator who doesn't know or understand the culture of the school. The second scenario involves an administrator who has been at the school for a number of years but fails to consider the culture of the school when designing strategies to implement a reform initiative.

Simply put, culture refers to "the way we do things around here." School culture reflects how long the school has been in existence (those pesky traditions!); how long the staff has been there; who the major players are on the staff; norms; past practices; belief systems; and what is valued, honored, and celebrated at the school. Jerry L. Thacker and William D. McInerney (1992) found a significant correlation between school culture and student achievement, thereby making the case that principals *must* consider the school culture as part of the overall process of developing and beginning any reform initiative.

What *Is* Organizational Culture?

The culture of a school is often the mirror of the local community culture. Moving a school through a reform process requires a change in the attitudes, values, and beliefs of the external environment, as well as the school. The culture of a school has a direct impact on the success or failure of the implementation of a reform initiative.

Patterson, Purkey, and Parker (1986) provide a summary of information on the impact of school culture:

- School culture does affect the behavior and achievement of elementary and secondary school students (though the effect of classroom and student variables remains greater).
- School culture does not fall from the sky; it is created and thus can be manipulated by people within the school.
- School cultures are unique—whatever their commonalities, no two schools will be exactly alike, nor should they be.
- To the extent that it provides a focus and clear purpose for the school, culture becomes the cohesion that bonds the school together as it goes about its mission.
- Though we concentrate on its beneficial nature, culture can be counterproductive and an obstacle to educational success; culture can also be oppressive and discriminatory for various subgroups within the school.
- Lasting fundamental change (e.g., changes in teaching practice or the decision-making structure) requires understanding and, often, altering the school's culture; cultural change is a slow process.

The culture of a school organization is made up of the core values and beliefs that drive the behavior of individuals within that organization. The culture can be either positive or negative, and consequently can work for you or against you. The culture of an organization has a tremendous influence on how people will react to outside initiatives. Needless to say, this will be especially difficult if the initiative is contrary to the underlying beliefs, values, assumptions, and rewarded behaviors of the school culture. A current example is the cultural struggle between the notion of "*All* students can learn" espoused in the *No Child Left Behind Act* of 2001, and the historically culturally embedded notion in many schools that all students can learn *if* they are academically at grade level, can speak English, have no learning disabilities, have parents who support the work of the schools, are self-motivated and self-disciplined, attend school regularly, and do their homework.

It is imperative that the principal understand the school's culture and how it evolved. This is even more essential during a time of change, and it can be considered a critical, and often overlooked, attribute of the change process. These core beliefs and values act as a lens for people within the organization to evaluate and shape a change initiative into what they perceive it should be. The best-intentioned principal will have little success unless he or she is able to understand the school's culture at a deep level and has the skills to shape that culture to encourage people to change their behavior.

Often, a principal will first try to change the *attitudes and beliefs* of the faculty as the primary goal in changing the school culture. As Rick DuFour (2003) points out, the attitudes will probably be the last thing to change. The reason: past experiences result in current beliefs; beliefs reflect attitudes. In order to change beliefs and attitudes, it will be necessary to provide opportunities to gain new and positive experiences, thereby resulting in new or revised beliefs and, eventually, attitudes. This means that the culture cannot change *unless people change their current behaviors*. Recent studies have shown that many reform initiatives fail because the leadership has not addressed the beliefs, attitudes, and values of the stakeholders, reflected as the culture of the school. The strategic planning process (see Chapter 3) begins with an examination of the shared beliefs of all school stakeholders.

The physical representation of the culture of an organization may be found in the artifacts that represent "the way things are done around here." These may include bell schedules, assembly topics, slogans, discipline handbooks and suspension forms, teacher evaluation documents, and so forth. The principal has the opportunity to create and support new artifacts as the school culture begins to evolve and change to align with the shared vision of improving student achievement. What are some of the artifacts at your school that represent the school culture? And what do they say about your school?

Key Components of a School's Culture

So, how *do* you begin to explore and define a school's culture? *The Framework for Analysis of School Culture* (California Department of

Education, nd.) identifies some specific elements that contribute to the definition of a school's culture. These include Heroes and Heroines; Communication Network; Rites and Rituals; Lore and Myths; Rules, Rewards, and Sanctions; and Physical Environment. These elements are a valuable tool to assist in developing a clear understanding of the culture of a school. The following section will explore each element in greater depth.

Heroes and Heroines

The "heroes and heroines" of a school are those individuals who are recognized as role models that exemplify the organization's traditions, values, and beliefs. They are looked up to by other members of the staff and generally set the tone for "the way we do things around here." Examples might include the long-standing head football coach; a counselor who is actively involved in providing college counseling to students; and a foreign language teacher who mentors new teachers on taking attendance, making out grade reports, and so forth.

Communication Network

Every organization has an instantaneous (and often accurate) communication network. How often have you heard a "rumor" from the teachers' grapevine about a major (and highly confidential) decision at the district office level, and two weeks later it turned out to be true? The communication network is a complex system through which information is transmitted and interpreted throughout the organization. It represents a hierarchy and circulates the "truth" by which people are judged. People talk! So, how can you use that fact to your advantage?

There are various roles within the communication network. Each has value in keeping you, and everyone else, informed. By consciously identifying these people in the organization, the principal can begin to shape the culture of the school.

1. *Storytellers:* The values and beliefs of people within an organization are reinforced through stories about people and events. Stories send messages, both positive and negative, about the history of the organization and the way things are done. Stories have a profound impact on the people within the organization and on their beliefs about their own or the organization's effectiveness. The storytellers have a unique role in that they interpret what goes on in the organization and

transmit that interpretation through stories to reinforce cultural beliefs, both positive and negative. They can transmit valuable information to the principal about the culture of the organization, and provide a "weather vane" as the reform initiative progresses.

2. *Spies:* These are the individuals who know everything about everybody, and constantly gather information about what is happening within the organization. It is important for them to be "in the know" before everyone else. If someone has concerns about a particular issue, the spy will know who, what, and why. This person will sometimes drop by just to give the principal a "heads up."

3. *Priests/Priestesses:* Within every organization, there are individuals who guard the cultural values. Highly respected by the members of the organization, they are often consulted by others to ensure their actions are consistent with the values of the school culture. They are sometimes perceived as negative because they bring up all the reasons something cannot be done (if it goes against the current beliefs and values of the school culture). Once a principal has identified the priests and priestesses, it would be prudent to ensure at least one of these individuals is on the planning and implementation committees.

4. *Whisperers:* Sometimes described as the "unseen powers behind the throne," these individuals provide specific information about what will work or not, and why.

5. *Cabals:* Cabals refer to groups of two or more individuals who join forces around a common purpose. Cabals can be positive or negative, depending on the purpose that brings the individuals together. They may be the two or three teachers who step forward to take a leadership role in developing and implementing a piece of the reform initiative. They could also be made up of the saboteurs of the process.

Rites and Rituals

Every organization, whether it is religious, political, or social, has a set of structured, predictable activities and daily events (rituals) that reflect "the way we do things around here." Think of the various processes and procedures instituted at your school: attendance procedures, discipline policies and procedures, employee hiring procedures, evaluation processes, student activities such as assemblies, new student orientation, parents' night, college information night, and athletics. These rituals are reflective of the core values and beliefs of the organization. They lend value to the organization by providing clarity, a common identity, and a sense of security to the stakeholders about "the way we do things around here."

Rites, on the other hand, provide the vehicle for celebrating what is important to individuals within the organization. Some examples of rites include student of the month, teacher of the year, new faculty luncheons, homecoming, report cards, special athletic or yearbook assemblies, and graduation. In considering the culture of your school, you might ask yourself, "Do we have ways to celebrate improved student achievement for all students, or do we only celebrate the achievement of those who are academically already at the top?"

Effective principals retain ceremonies and rituals that support the reform effort, and begin to create new ceremonies and rituals as well. For example, rather than recognize only honor roll students at an honors assembly, the principal might incorporate recognition awards from each academic department for most improved student performance within those subject areas. Over time, this becomes an established part of the school culture. Thus, the principal begins the process of shaping the culture of the school to align with a shared vision around improving student achievement.

Lore and Myths

The culture of any organization is transmitted through stories about "the way we do things around here." They provide the historical context of the school culture. There are stories about the school as the football powerhouse that won the state championship back in 1985, the nationally ranked music program, and the medical career academy that sends 95% of its students to college or university programs. How often have you heard someone say, "But we've *always* done it that way;" "If it ain't broke, don't fix it;" or, "We tried that 15 years ago. It didn't work then and it won't work now." These statements are often accompanied by stories that support the speaker's position, for example, the bell schedule that allows teachers to socialize and/or collaborate during the single lunch period, but resulted in a very large number of students being tardy for their 4th-period classes. Or how the teachers voted on a tardy lockout policy that resulted in a reduction in interruptions during instructional time, but caused an unacceptable number of students to miss critical instruction. Another example might be how the school tried block scheduling in years past but discontinued it because the teachers had difficulty keeping the students' attention while they lectured for 90 minutes straight.

Knowing that stories are an essential and valued component of the organizational culture, principals can begin to reshape the culture of the school by developing and telling stories about staff, students, school organizations, data, and projects to illustrate shared beliefs and values that support the direction of the reform efforts.

Myths, on the other hand, are beliefs that are deeply embedded within the culture and have evolved to an almost mystical status based on many years of retelling. Myths, by definition, are not based on reality or truth, but support the beliefs of the myth-teller. The belief is often contrary to the assumptions inherent in reform efforts such as the *No Child Left Behind Act* of 2001. Many of the following myths identified in the Massachusetts Institute of Technology report *Education That Works: An Action Plan for the Education of Minorities* (Quality Education for Minorities Project, 1990, p. 3) prevail in secondary schools today:

- Learning is due to innate abilities, and minorities are simply less capable of educational excellence than whites. (p. 37)
- The situation is hopeless; the problems minority youth face . . . are so overwhelming that society is incapable of providing effective responses. (p. 37)
- Quality education for all is a luxury, since not all jobs presently require creativity and problem-solving skills. (p. 38)
- Education is an expense and not an investment. (p. 38)
- Equity and excellence in education are in conflict. (p. 38)
- All we need are marginal changes. (p. 39)
- Minorities don't care about education. (p. 39)
- The problem will go away. (p. 40)
- Educational success or failure is within the complete control of each individual, and in America anybody can make it. (p. 40)

Effective principals listen to and strive to understand the source of the myths, while clearly articulating those stories that illustrate and support the vision of improving the achievement of all students. A primary role of the principal is to provide a forum for stakeholders to identify and confront myths within the school's culture that impede the ability of all students to make significant academic gains. It is the leadership responsibility of the principal to provide current research, information, and resources to stakeholders involved in the reform process to facilitate the resolution of inherent fears and anxieties, and support the behavioral changes necessary to create new attitudes and beliefs.

Rules, Rewards, and Sanctions

Every organization has an implied set of behavioral expectations, or norms, for its members about "how we do business around here." These rules impact our behavior within the context of the organization. Members of an organization either reward or sanction these behaviors based upon their alignment with the rules/norms of the organization.

Physical Environment

The physical location of classrooms and offices reflects the culture of the school. If you want to make a clerical staff member angry, move the staff member out of his or her office and into a smaller office on the other side of the building. If all the special education classes are in portable classrooms on the far side of campus next to the football stadium, what does that say about the beliefs and values of the school relative to students with disabilities? If the school is sparkling clean or covered with trash and dirt, what does that say about how the staff and students feel about their school? Effective secondary principals pay attention to the physical environment as a visible indicator of the culture of the school.

Research has indicated that if these cultural elements are not addressed, reform efforts will fail. Effective secondary principals consciously identify, incorporate, and use these cultural elements throughout the change process.

What the Research Says About Cultural Norms That Facilitate School Improvement

The research article *School Context: Bridge or Barrier to Change?* (Boyd, 1992) provides an in-depth review of research findings around school culture. A basic finding of various writers indicates that in order for a change effort to be successful, cultural norms that support the change effort must be in place. The following cultural norms are critical to success:

- A norm of protecting what is important, which is a direct result of having a vision of what is important shared by staff, students, and the community
- The norm of a school's continuous critical inquiry of its strengths and weaknesses as a basis for reform, as well as a willingness to continually adapt, experiment, and reinvent it

- The norm of continuous improvement that ensures that access to information, resources, and technical support will be provided to address any problems or challenges that arise
- The norm of active participation in the decision-making process by those who are directly and indirectly affected by the reform effort (Boyd, p. 9).

During this era of high-stakes accountability in the reform of public schools, secondary principals should systematically address the issue of changing the school culture if it is contrary to the goals set forth in the school's action plan.

Case Studies

The following case studies illustrate the impact of school culture on initiating and implementing reform efforts. The first case study illustrates the actions taken to improve student achievement at an older high school with strong school traditions. The second case study illustrates issues faced by a middle school moving through major shifts in student diversity and the principal's actions to address reform mandates.

 ## Case Study 1: Working With Strong Traditional School Culture

Municipal High School

Anna S. was named as principal of Municipal High School the previous year after serving as a co-administrator at a middle school. Seventy years old, Municipal High School is viewed as the flagship school of the district, reflecting strong community traditions and expectations. Many of the mostly white, middle-class faculty have been there for over 25 years and had, in fact, graduated from the school. Their teaching strategies tend to be very traditional, and reflect a belief that all students can learn based on their innate ability or aptitude. Although they believe that it is their responsibility to provide clear and engaging lessons, it is ultimately up to the students to take advantage of the opportunity to learn. If they choose not to learn, the faculty honors that decision. The school culture encompasses strong traditions, high expectations, and a "survival of the fittest" mentality.

Over the years, the demographics of the school have changed from a predominantly white, rural population to a culturally diverse racial and ethnic student population made up of 48% African Americans, 27% Hispanic students, 20% Caucasians, and 5% other ethnic minorities. The student population also includes 75% of students on free and reduced lunch (thereby qualifying the school for Schoolwide Title I status), 28% in the English Language Learners program, and 25% in special education programs. The school is in its third year as a designated underperforming high school based on AYP (Adequate Yearly Progress) factors, specifically, the failure of all subgroups to meet minimal performance levels. The school has a 52% transiency rate. Gang activity and school safety are relevant issues.

Anna was selected for the position due to her belief that all students can learn, as well as the plan that she developed to move the reform agenda forward. However, Anna recognizes that the school has a strong and pervasive culture and tradition of meeting the educational needs of those students who are already motivated, self-disciplined, and college-bound. She initiated some specific strategies to promote the major changes in the school's culture that had to occur to move the reform agenda forward.

Prior to the opening of school, Anna made a point to talk to co-administrators, parents, students, department chairs, secretaries and clerical staff, custodians, security staff, and any teachers who happened to be at the school during the summer. During these conversations, she specifically began to identify the traditions, routines, rules, beliefs, and myths, as well as the priests and priestesses, heroes and heroines, and other key stakeholders at the school.

At the initial meeting of faculty and staff prior to the opening of school, Anna displayed the school's AYP results and clearly articulated her belief that the students could improve their achievement through the institution of a standards-based instructional program, as required by the state and the district. She invited all staff to collaborate in the development of a shared vision and school plan that emphasized the academic achievement of all students. The message of improving the academic achievement of all students and the mandate of improving test scores was also delivered to the staff by the superintendent and a school board member.

During the next two days, all staff members were given an opportunity within departmental groups to review the State Academic Content Standards in language arts and mathematics, and identify those standards that could be addressed within their own content areas. These lists were turned in to Anna, who requested that all teachers incorporate these "common standards" into their own curriculum and specify how they would address them as part of their required goals and objectives for the year.

After issuing a general invitation to all staff members, Anna personally invited key stakeholders to participate on a School Leadership Team, being especially careful to include some of the "priests and priestesses" to bring forth issues related to current traditions and expectations versus the realities of moving the reform agenda forward. She hired an outside coach to facilitate the process. She also invited the school's bargaining unit representative, a district office director, and a school board member to participate in the planning process. The planning committee, composed of teachers, classified staff members, students, parents, and community members, met monthly for 2 to 4 hours over the first year. Initial operating norms were established; outcomes were specified; and a timeline was determined. At the first meeting, stakeholders engaged in an activity to identify their own beliefs and values and the cultural norms of the school. Because of the intensity of the discussion, this initial process took two months to complete. Anna was an active participant in the process and provided parameters within the scope of the state and district mandates.

With ongoing input by staff, students, and parent/community groups, the School Leadership Team created a shared vision statement that formed the basis for a comprehensive school plan. They considered district and schoolwide student performance data, and examined a wide variety of additional data about the school (see Chapter 3, The Single School Plan). They assessed the school's traditions, policies, procedures, programs, and routines that represent the existing cultural reality, and systematically incorporated those that supported the reform agenda.

Recognizing the critical importance of providing necessary support and resources to facilitate a change in the school's culture, Anna recruited four full-time release instructional coaches (English/Language Arts and Social Studies, Math and Science, Special Populations, and Electives) to provide ongoing support and assistance to departments throughout the reform process. Based on immediate teacher concerns and requests, she also provided additional funds to each teacher for supplies, access to duplicating machines, and Saturday workshops on how to effectively use the newly acquired language arts texts and resource materials.

Anna clearly communicated to the staff the expectation that they teach to the State Academic Standards. This expectation was translated into the professional goals and objectives for each teacher. Evaluative data was collected through the teacher evaluation process outlined in the bargaining unit contract. She initiated a protocol for frequent nonevaluative classroom "drop-ins" by administrators, district office staff, and peers, with a focus on teaching to the State Academic Standards. Mini workshop sessions that outlined the process and the criteria were made available to all stakeholders participating in the "walk-throughs" (see Chapter 8, Productive Classroom Observations). This action was taken to address the existing cultural norm of teacher isolation and "doing your own thing" in the classroom.

Based on stated school goals and a survey that identified the differentiated learning needs of her faculty, Anna and a group of teacher leaders and instructional coaches developed a professional development plan that was incorporated into the single school plan. This plan provided immediate and long-term professional development opportunities on cultural diversity, teaching to state standards, using assessment data to inform instruction, effective instructional practices, reflective practice, and peer coaching. The plan reflected a comprehensive and sustained professional development effort that included dedicated time for learning conversations, collaborative department meetings around student learning issues based on benchmark data, and three mini-workshop series on topics specific to stated school goals.

At the fourth staff meeting, Anna instituted the first monthly "Teacher of the Month" recognition, with an award certificate, a donated dinner-for-two gift certificate, and positive "testimonials" by staff and students. Nominated by students, parents, and/or staff, honored teachers reflected actions and beliefs that personified the direction of the reform efforts. Teachers were encouraged to share success stories during department meetings and at staff meetings. The "successes" illustrated ways that identified issues/problems were addressed in the classroom. Time was available on the agendas for this to occur in small groups or through individual presentations to the full staff.

It should be noted that Anna's first year was very difficult and time consuming. Many staff members struggled through the initiation of the reform process, feeling overwhelmed by the new information and expectations, and grieving for the loss of the existing school culture. Not all stakeholders willingly participated in the various activities. During the first quarter, there were midnight calls to board members and the superintendent, complaints to the bargaining unit president, and requests for transfers to other schools. Anna happily approved these transfer requests and actively recruited new staff members who expressed the beliefs and values necessary for the reform efforts. She maintained an open communication system with the district and teachers' association leadership, to address anticipated concerns and keep the leadership informed throughout the process. She also spent considerable time building personal relationships with staff, parents, and students through her open-door policy, as well as her visibility and availability during lunch and passing periods, before and after school, and at key parent, student, and individual meetings with staff. By the end of the first semester, things began to settle down as staff members had a clearer idea of the vision, obtained needed support, and began to see the impact in their own classrooms.

Points to Consider

- Effective principals, co-administrators, and instructional leaders model the values and beliefs that are important to the school, and encourage teachers and students to do the same. These actions result in a clear message to everyone about "what is important." Walk the talk!
- Work collaboratively with teachers, staff, students, and parents to develop a shared vision based on beliefs, values, and historical context. Be prepared for this process to take some time.
- Consider getting an outside facilitator for the development of a vision statement and strategic plan. There is no doubt that conversations during this process will unearth some major differences in stakeholder beliefs and values. This can be messy. Stay the course!
- Acknowledge up front that there will be major differences and conflicts among stakeholders. Discuss and establish norms to set safe parameters for the conversations.
- Use storytelling at staff meetings, committee meetings, community forums, and parent meetings to spotlight shared values and beliefs.
- Create new heroes and heroines by telling stories about their "heroic" accomplishments, adventures, and activities.
- Invite the priests and priestesses to participate in the decision-making process, thereby giving them the opportunity to interpret new initiatives through the belief systems of the organization.
- Whenever possible, align new ideas with the historical record of "what works here."
- Develop a cultural norm of shared decision making. This will require the principal to be flexible with his or her agenda within the constraints of current mandates.
- Recruit, retain, and reward staff members who share the beliefs, values, and behaviors required to move the reform agenda forward.

- Be prepared for conflict, opposition, and sabotage; change cannot happen without it! Don't take things personally (and that's not always easy to do!).
- Develop and maintain strong communication links with the district and bargaining unit leadership. This will assist in identifying potential problems or issues up front, provide accurate information to counter the whisperers who try to sabotage your efforts, and generally facilitate the planning and implementation process.

 Case Study 2: Working With a Diversifying Student Body

Greenview Middle School

Mary, a white, former math teacher at the school, is beginning her first year as principal of Greenview Middle School following three years as a co-administrator. Greenview Middle School is comprised of approximately 1200 seventh- and eighth-grade students. The student population is made up of 40% Caucasian, 35% Hispanic, 10% Asian, 10% African-American, and 5% other ethnic students. Ten percent of the students are enrolled in special education classes and 35% of the students are Limited English Proficient. The school is a designated Schoolwide Title I school due to the large percentage of students in the free and reduced lunch program, and is in its third year as a designated program improvement school based on Adequate Yearly Progress (AYP) results. Recently, the school was designated as an Unsafe School through NCLB (*No Child Left Behind Act* of 2001) due to its excessive number of expulsions.

Ten years old, the school is made up of a cadre of veteran white, middle-class faculty members who tend to be traditional in their teaching strategies; many of them have been passed over for teaching assignments at the high school. The faculty expresses frustration in dealing with student behaviors that reflect the racial and ethnic changes in the student population and frequently refers students to the vice principal for actions such as "rolling their eyes." As a vice principal, Mary supported teachers in maintaining a strong culture of student discipline, resulting in the largest number of school expulsions in the county during the previous year.

The faculty holds a general belief that all students can learn and demonstrate some growth based upon their innate ability or aptitudes and effort. The faculty provides multiple opportunities for students to learn. Although students are encouraged to learn, whether they do or not is dependent upon external factors such as degree of parent support, socioeconomic status, and internal motivation, which are considered beyond the control of the faculty.

Because Mary is so efficient and task oriented, she completed the school plan during the summer prior to the beginning of school and presented it to the faculty at the beginning of the year. She did not elicit input during the writing of the plan, depending solely on her firsthand knowledge of the staff and school issues as well as the culture of the school. The plan was quite directive and included specific goals, strategies, and performance indicators, along with timelines for implementation. Mary decided to retain full responsibility for plan implementation monitoring since she was not confident that the staff was capable of getting the job done. Every teacher was required to incorporate the objectives, activities, and timelines into his or her annual "goals and objectives" document.

Almost immediately, Mary began receiving complaints from the faculty, parents, students, and some community members about changes she had incorporated into the plan and initiated. Many teachers refused to attend staff development sessions designed to change their instructional practices, as well as develop knowledge and skills to address the diverse student population, citing the teachers' contract language. In the meantime, stories began to circulate within the school, the district, and in the surrounding community of the "disastrous" changes that threatened the sacred traditions of the school and were being imposed from above. By the end of the first semester, Mary's doctor had doubled her blood pressure medication and the superintendent was considering putting her on an assistance plan.

Points to Consider

- Don't assume that you alone know the beliefs, values, assumptions, and cultural priorities of the school. *Including all stakeholders in the process is essential.*
- Changing the culture of an organization is a journey, not an end product. It is *the* most difficult part of change. Be patient but persistent.
- Developing, monitoring, and revising the plan is an ongoing, systematic process; it is part of the journey! Don't think you are finished when the plan is developed.
- Communication systems can work for you or against you, depending on how you utilize them (or not!).

Summary

The culture of an organization is represented by the beliefs, values, and attitudes of the people in the organization, and is reflected in "how we do things around here." Establishing a vision for school reform is the first step in the long and challenging journey of the reform process. This is particularly necessary if the existing culture and norms of the school are contrary to the mission of educational reform. Identifying the key members of the communication network and analyzing the various cultural elements, such as the stories, reward and sanction system, and existing rites and rituals, will provide a starting point in initiating and facilitating behavior changes that will ultimately result in changes in beliefs and values of stakeholders. This process requires strong leadership and persistence by the instructional leaders of the school.

Application Activity

1. Thinking about your own staff, who are the individuals that might fall within each of the categories of the Communication Network?

2. What are some of the rites and rituals at your school that demonstrate what is important to people within the organization?

3. What are some of the artifacts from your school that would provide indicators of the school culture?

4. What are some basic operational norms or agreements for staff behavior that you would like to have in place at your school?

2

The Change
Process

Change Is Your Friend!

There is no question that we live in a culture of complex and
fast-moving change. The explosion in technological advances, increasing
social diversity, transiency, and unstable economic factors exacerbate
this culture of change. In addition, a school leader must acknowledge
the enormity of change taking place in education, be knowledgeable of
the change research, and use available tools for managing and facilitating the change process.

A key to being an effective instructional leader is the ability to
articulate a clear vision for school improvement. Moreover, it is
important that each stakeholder envision his or her role in achieving
the school vision. In order to lead effective school reform in secondary
schools, the principal must provide opportunities for the school
leadership, as well as the staff, to answer the following questions:

- Why is this reform effort needed?
- Is this good for students?
- What impact will this change have on me?
- What is my role in this effort to improve student achievement?
- What do I have to do to ensure this reform effort occurs?
- How will I know that my efforts are making a difference?

Within the field of education, principals and other instructional leaders are faced with the challenge of meeting the demands of parents, the community, politicians, and the district office administration for improving student achievement at all levels. The Adequate Yearly Progress (AYP) requirement of the *No Child Left Behind Act* of 2001 (NCLB) for schools and districts is an example of a national mandate for increased student performance accountability. Predictably, not everyone at the school site eagerly embraces the notion of changing what he or she is doing to meet this challenge.

Principles of the Change Process

Since the late 1970s, there have been extensive research and exploration of this thing we call the change process. What happens to systems and, more importantly, to people during periods of major change and innovation? Too often, brilliant action plans crash in flames due primarily to the failure of key stakeholders to fully understand the process. Even more damaging is the failure of principals, co-administrators, and other instructional leaders to provide appropriate support to those who *do* engage in the process, due to a basic lack of understanding about how to apply the principles of the change process. As our understanding of the effects of change on different stakeholders emerges through ongoing research efforts, effective principals and other instructional leaders are able to apply this knowledge to maximize the participation of stakeholders, provide appropriate support throughout the process, ensure success in institutionalizing reform efforts, and, most importantly, improve student achievement.

Fullan and Hargreaves (1991) have written extensively on the impact of change within organizations. They have identified four key strands in managing change: the Change Process, Culture of the School, Teacher Development, and School/Community Relationships. Subsequent chapters in this book will touch on each of these strands. For change to become institutionalized, a transformation of the organizational culture must occur. This process is complex, difficult, and messy. However, substantive change cannot occur without moving through the process with enthusiasm, courage, and hope.

Throughout this chapter, the term "innovation" is used to describe anything that is new to the culture of the school, such as an emphasis on Explicit Direct Instruction, cooperative learning, teaching to standards, the use of rubrics, or implementing a new library software system.

Fullan and Hargreaves (1991) have developed a model that describes the phases of the change process within an organization as follows:

Phase 1, the Initiation Phase: This is described as "the process leading up to and including the decision to proceed with implementation of a change" (Fullan & Hargreaves, 1991, p. 50). This critical phase requires adequate time to assess "relevance, readiness, and resources" necessary for moving forward with the innovation. This phase also requires opportunities for input and participation by all those who will be expected to participate in the change effort. Listed below are some practices outlined by Jody Westbrook and Valarie Spiser-Albert (2002) that will assist in successful implementation of Phase 1:

- Everyone who will be involved with implementing the change should be involved early in the planning process.
- Those leading the change process should answer questions without judgment or defensiveness.
- Those leading the change process should address the concerns of others.
- Those implementing the change should be provided with adequate resources such as time, materials, and financial support. (p. 15)

Phase 2, the Implementation Phase: During this phase, the change agent is putting new programs, activities, or structures into practice. Some of the activities inherent in this phase include vision development, building initiative, empowering stakeholders, assisting others through professional development and providing resources, and monitoring (formative assessment). Problem solving occurs as issues are identified, and continues beyond the planning process as the change progresses into implementation. Practices that support the implementation of Phase 2 include the following:

- Clarify what the new practice should look like when fully implemented and how it will look as it progresses.
- Communicate clearly the expect timeline for full implementation.
- Provide a relationship between evaluators and implementers that includes some coaching and observations without evaluation. (Westbrook & Spiser-Albert, 2002, p. 18)

Phase 3, Institutionalization: During this phase, the change is fully in place and has become part of the culture of the organization. It is important to stress that there will continue to be a need for support, resources, and time to ensure the continuation of the change effort. If the change effort is not continually emphasized as important, there is the possibility that it will be abandoned over time.

Fullan (2001) has identified some key principles of change that every administrator should know and consider on a daily basis. Some of the change principles that should be considered as part of the planning process, and incorporated and reviewed often during the implementation of the change effort, are as follows:

- Change is a process, not a blueprint. Too often in education, some type of innovation is introduced without considering what needs to happen within the organization to effectively implement it. As a site administrator, it is critical to consider the implementation process as an ongoing challenge based upon the progress of each individual stakeholder.

- Change takes time. Research indicates it takes from 3 to 5 years for change to become institutionalized. For larger organizations (think of statewide initiatives) it takes even longer. Too often, districts and schools jump from one innovation to another without recognizing that the previous innovation is still going through the process. This results in failure, burnout (from excessive "innovations du jour"), and a general cynicism about change. It's important to recognize the time commitment and build it into the planning process.

- Change is personal and is different for each individual based upon his or her experiences, beliefs, and values. Each individual must establish his or her own meaning of the innovation. It will be necessary to include a wide range of risk-free opportunities within the process for this to occur.

- The change that actually occurs will not look like the one you may have originally envisioned. Any change initiative tends to "morph" into something unique to your own organization, based upon the beliefs, values, and experiences of those going through the process (Hall & Hord, 2001).

- Conflict and disagreements are inevitable. They are also essential to the change process as different perspectives are considered. Look upon these conflicts and disagreements as opportunities to problem solve and plan, rather than excuses for nonparticipation.

- Things often get worse before they get better. Fullan points to the "Implementation Dip," during which anticipated results (e.g., test scores) often go down before they start to go back up when an innovation is introduced, requiring new skills and knowledge (p. 40).
- Don't expect all (or even most) of the people or groups to change at the beginning of the process. Start with the willing and take steps to increase the number of participants over time.
- No amount of frontloading knowledge or information will ever result in a clear path of action to be taken. Sometimes you just need to move ahead in planning and action, with the understanding that you may need to go back and modify at a later time.
- People need pressure to change, even in directions they support. Principals should articulate and demonstrate a clear expectation that stakeholders fully participate in the process. The key is to take steps that allow people to move through the process at their own rate, react, form their own positions, interact with others, receive technical assistance, and so forth (see Stages of Concern, Figure 2.1, and Levels of Use, Figure 2.2), thus increasing participation over time.
- Don't try to institute too many changes/innovations at one time. This results in overload, dissonance, and general burnout (Fullan, 2001, p. 36).

(For further resources by Michael Fullan, please see the reference list.)

Concerns-Based Adoption Model (CBAM)

This chapter emphasizes the Concerns-Based Adoption Model (CBAM), developed by Gene Hall and Susan Loucks-Horsely in the early 1970s at the University of Texas Educational Research Center, and continually refined and researched since that time. This research focuses on the dynamics that occur when an individual moves through the process of learning new skills and knowledge. As individuals, we are constantly learning new skills: e.g., how to drive a stick shift, how to use a computer or new software program, how to bake bread, how to play an instrument, or how to play golf. *The process we go through is quite predictable and represents the stages of the change process.* This model demonstrates the stages or phases that a person goes through when attempting to implement any change.

Knowing the model and how to recognize the stages is only part of the equation. The key to being an effective principal, co-administrator, or other instructional leader is to apply this information in the planning, implementation, and assessment of any innovation that is initiated by the school during the reform efforts that characterize schools today.

What Is CBAM?

The Concerns-Based Adoption Model (CBAM) is an organizational structure that describes what happens within an organization when a change occurs. It is composed of the Innovation Configuration, Stages of Concern, and Levels of Use. The Concern-Based Adoption Model is based on the premise that change is a personal and highly individual process. When learning a new skill, people progress through a series of very predictable stages at their own rate and in their own way, based on their beliefs, values, and past experiences (see Figure 2.1 Stages of Concern, and Figure 2.2 Levels of Use). This book will examine the Stages of Concern (SOC) and the Levels of Use (LOU) as informal assessment tools to assist school leaders in gathering formative data throughout the implementation of a reform effort.

SOC and LOU stages cannot be skipped. However, due to current reform mandates, many teachers are being required to move straight into Routine and Refinement (see Figure 2.2 Levels of Use) practices without the benefit of the preliminary information and support they should receive in the earlier stages. In reality, how long a person stays at a particular level, or how long it takes to progress to the next level, is an individual choice. Coercion doesn't work! Appropriate support based on the needs of the individual *does* work!

Stages of Concern (SOC)

The Stages of Concern describe the concerns, feelings, or perceptions of individuals as they progress through the challenges of implementing something new. The seven stages are broken down into the following four categories:

- **Awareness** refers to people who have limited or no knowledge of the innovation.
- **Self** refers to a concern about how the innovation will impact them on a personal level.

Figure 2.1 Stages of Concern (SOC)

Category	Stage	Name	Description
Awareness	0	Awareness	The person is neither concerned about nor involved in the innovation.
Awareness	1	Informational	The person has a general awareness and is interested in acquiring more detailed information about the innovation. Specifically, the concern is around what "it" looks like and how to use "it."
Self	2	Personal	The person is concerned about how the innovation will impact him or her and existing routines, responsibilities, and practices, as well as his or her own adequacy in implementation. There is an emphasis on his or her own role relative to decision making, potential conflict, personal commitment, financial and status implications, and the reward structure of the organization. In other words, "How will this impact *me?*"
Task	3	Management	The person is concerned about the time needed for preparation, difficulty in moving through steps, and general lack of expertise in the innovation. Emphasis centers on efficiency, organization, and management.
Impact	4	Consequence	The person is concerned about the impact of the innovation on his or her students or those who are within his or her sphere of influence. The emphasis is on relevance to students, evaluation of the outcomes, and changes that will facilitate improved student performance.
Impact	5	Collaboration	The person is concerned about how to relate what he or she is doing with what other instructors are doing. Emphasis is on collaboration and cooperation to improve student performance.
Impact	6	Refocusing	The person develops major changes based upon the exploration of more universal benefits of the innovation. He or she may also begin to develop new ideas and strategies that will work even better.

Adapted from *Implementing Change: Patterns, Principles, and Potholes*, by G. E. Hall and S. M. Hord, 2001, Boston: Allyn & Bacon.

- **Task** refers to changes they will have to make within their current operational structures as they build knowledge, understanding, and skills.
- **Impact** refers to concerns around the impact of the innovation on students, how to enhance results through active collaboration with colleagues, and how to adapt and refine the innovation for maximum effectiveness.

Levels of Use (LOU)

Levels of Use refers to what the individual is actually doing relative to using and implementing the innovation. It is important to understand that these levels address the notion of free will and choice. Individuals must internally decide that they will use the innovation in order to progress.

There are two major decision points within the LOU configuration (see Figure 2.2, Levels of Use). The first comes after the Preparation and before Mechanical Use stages. At this point, it is possible to acquire information about an innovation and even begin to gather the necessary materials and resources. However, this does not mean that the person has actually made a commitment to actively participate in the reform. (For example, some people may seek out information about computers and even buy one, but never actually use the computer.)

The second decision point comes after the Routine Use stage, at which point the individual is comfortable with and reasonably proficient in the use of the innovation. During this stage, the impact on students is not a consideration in planning and implementation. The focus is on the comfort level of the teacher in the use of the innovation.

During the shift to the Refinement stage, the individual must overtly begin to focus on how the innovation impacts students as a new lens for planning and implementation. Current reform mandates require that teachers consider student performance data to inform instruction. This use of student performance data is a Refinement stage activity. It is critical that administrators and instructional leaders understand that teachers are still moving through the Mechanical and Routine stages with the curriculum standards, new textbooks, implementation and analysis of formative and summative assessment data, and instructional practices being implemented as part of the reform efforts under the *No Child Left Behind Act* of 2001.

These two decision points are internally activated, although external conditions may be structured to facilitate the process. For example, if there is an expectation of use, this may be factored into the goals and

Figure 2.2 Levels of Use (LOU)

Stage	Name	Description
0	Non-use	The person is not using or addressing the innovation.
1	Orientation	The person is acquiring information about the innovation through articles, information meetings, workshops, etc.
2	Preparation	The person is gathering the needed information, materials, and resources, as well as planning to begin use.
Decision Point The individual establishes a date and time to begin use.		
3	Mechanical	The person is implementing the innovation. Initially, a step-by-step process is carefully followed, there are occasional instances of failure, and participants spend a significant amount of time planning and gathering materials and resources.
4a	Routine	The person has become more comfortable with the innovation and is able to implement without the major time commitments required during the Mechanical Stage. The focus is on the comfort level of the individual, not on the impact on students.
Decision Point The focus shifts from the individual to the student.		
4b	Refinement	The person begins to plan and implement with a clear focus on improving the impact on students.
5	Integration	The person begins to actively seek out and collaborate with others on ways to improve the impact of the innovation on students.
6	Renewal	The innovation has become "internalized" within the person's instructional repertoire. Clearly expert in the innovation, the person begins to explore alternative ideas, strategies, methods, and innovations. Note: At this point, the change process begins again.

Adapted from *Implementing Change: Patterns, Principles, and Potholes*, by G. E. Hall and S. M. Hord, 2001, Boston: Allyn & Bacon.

objectives conferences at the beginning of the year. Discussions about use may be included in staff meetings, and opportunities for teachers to examine student work as a means of assessing impact on students may be part of the ongoing professional development structure. These measures facilitate, but do not ensure, active participation. The individual may choose to passively, rather than actively, participate. It's the old "You can lead a horse to water" conundrum.

Implementation Strategies

The authors acknowledge that there is no magic pill or completely effective checklist for leading a school reform effort. Change is complex and messy. As Michael Fullan noted, "It [understanding the change process] is less about strategy and more about strategizing" (2003, p. 31). The "Application Activities" included in this book present some key questions to consider and provide opportunities for principals and instructional leaders to reflect and begin to strategize. This reflecting and strategizing process should include representatives from all stakeholder groups to ensure the change effort is not simply "top down," but reflects a "top-down–bottom-up" approach as the school moves through the Initiation and Implementation phases.

Where do I start?

Planning for change based on a vision for improving student achievement is essential. Communicating this vision to all stakeholders, as well as eliciting stakeholder participation in the process, is also essential. During the Initiation Phase, which includes planning and initial implementation, Fullan and Hargreaves (1991) caution us to consider "relevance, readiness, and resources."

How will I know what stages people are in at any given time?

It's fairly easy to assess where people are in terms of use of the innovation just by noting what they are saying in conversation or on survey responses. Staff will provide you with clues as to the Level of Use stage they are experiencing. The following chart (Figure 2.3) provides some examples of what each level sounds like as you engage people in conversation or ask for written feedback on progress.

Hall and Hord (2001) refer to brief one-on-one conversations about the innovation as "one-legged conversations"—the conversations should only last about as long as you can stand on one leg. Opening questions could be as simple as, "How are you progressing with (reform)?" As you listen to responses, determine the level and what type of support is needed (see Figure 2.3).

Figure 2.3   What LOU Sounds Like

Stage	Name	What it sounds like
0	Non-Use	I don't know anything about it. I'm not doing/using (reform) in my classroom. I think I remember hearing someone mention this in the faculty lounge, or was it at a staff meeting?
1	Orientation	I've gone to an informational workshop and talked to two colleagues to see how they use it in their classes. Mary gave me a good article to read that provided a really clear explanation.
2	Preparation	I've attended a district workshop that outlined specific strategies that I can use. I'm also thinking about the materials I may need to do this in my classroom. I'm planning to try it out in a lesson next Monday.
3	Mechanical	I can't believe how long it takes me to plan each class. I worked all weekend. I tried something new today and it was a disaster! I'm still trying to figure out how to use all the materials.
4a	Routine	I've incorporated (reform) into most of my lessons now, and it seems to go pretty well. It doesn't take too much planning time anymore, and I don't have to search for materials all the time. It's working for me.
4b	Refinement	Although it seems to be working for most of the students, I've noticed that the special ed and EL students are not always successful in meeting the objectives. I've been looking for ways to increase the success for these students.
5	Integration	Our department has been bringing student work to our department meetings to discuss progress, issues, and strategies. I've also been talking to John and Sue about what they're doing with (reform) in their classrooms to ensure all the students are successful. We'd like to have some release time to observe each other's classes to pick up some ideas. Could that be arranged?
6	Renewal	I really love using (reform) in my classroom. I've been doing some workshops for other departments on strategies they can use and will be presenting at a state conference. Lately, I've been fascinated with this notion of brain research and how it integrates with (reform). I'm going to be doing more investigation along these lines.

Adapted from *Implementing Change: Patterns, Principles, and Potholes*, by G. E. Hall and S. M. Hord, 2001, Boston: Allyn & Bacon.

What is considered appropriate support at each stage?

Just recognizing the concerns about the reform initiative or the staff's Levels of Use is not enough. The next step is to provide your staff with support as they maneuver through that particular stage or level. The support that effective leaders provide is specific to the stage or level. It is not a one-size-fits-all model.

The stakeholders will not all be marching along at the same rate through the process. Consequently, as the instructional leader, it will be the principal's responsibility to ensure that a variety of support mechanisms are in place for those at different stages of the process. Since most of these mechanisms involve a financial commitment, it is important during the planning process to consider what support you will make available, to ensure funding sources are identified and funds are available. The following table (Figure 2.4, Appropriate Support Options for LOU Stages) provides suggestions for support at each level of the LOU.

How will I know we are moving forward with the change effort?

Any Single School Plan (see Chapter 3) should address the assessed needs of the school. Student summative test scores alone only tell the end result of the story. As the school leadership team begins the process of determining specific goals, objectives, and "steps," it is critical to assess the SOC/LOU of staff members, including the administration, relative to their beliefs and attitudes, as well as the understanding of curriculum standards, instructional strategies, and assessment strategies of individuals.

Possible data sources for acquiring information for assessing progress include the following:

- Disaggregated student achievement data (AYP data, standardized tests, teacher tests, benchmarks)
- Grade distribution analysis broken down by teacher
- Direct classroom observations
- The school budget
- Attendance data broken down by teacher
- Lesson plans
- Agendas and minutes from department and committee meetings
- Interviews with a focus on SOC and LOU
- Surveys and questionnaires
- Teacher/administrator portfolio reviews

Figure 2.4 Appropriate Support Options for LOU Stages

Stage	Name	Options for support
1	Non-Use	Individual informational conversations. Clearly state expectations to participate in the (reform).
2	Orientation	Informational meetings Overview presentations at staff meetings Books, magazines, articles Attendance at relevant conferences, workshops
3	Preparation	District workshops Site implementation workshops Release time for team planning and/or observations Materials, resources, equipment needed for implementation List of relevant Web sites
4a	Mechanical	Network meetings (weekly? monthly?) to discuss issues and problem solving in department/grade-level groups Peer coaching Release time to observe other teachers Materials, resources needed for implementation District/site implementation workshops—targeted topics List of relevant Web sites
4b	Routine	Opportunities to share experiences, resources, strategies at staff meetings, department meetings Release time to observe other teachers engage in (reform) activity Attendance at site, district, and outside workshops/conferences Opportunities for Action Research (see Chapter 7) Funds for books, magazines, articles about (reform) Opportunity to facilitate at network meetings List of relevant Web sites
5	Refinement	Opportunities to share experiences, resources, strategies at staff meetings, department meetings Release time for teachers to observe each other and engage in collaborative debriefing discussions Opportunities for Action Research Opportunities to serve as a peer coach Opportunities for collaboration at department meetings Opportunities to attend or present at site, district, and outside workshops/conferences
6	Renewal	Opportunities to present about (reform) at site, district, outside workshops/conferences Attendance at other related workshops or conferences of interest Funds for books, magazines, articles, software

Adapted from *Implementing Change: Patterns, Principles, and Potholes,* by G. E. Hall and S. M. Hord, 2001, Boston: Allyn & Bacon.

This data provides information necessary for setting student achievement targets, as well as the information required for establishing professional development goals outlined in the Single School Plan.

Ongoing assessment of progress will establish the success or failure of the staff in meeting identified goals. Data should continue to be collected throughout the year and analyzed at designated points to monitor progress and make necessary adaptations or modifications, as needed. Chapter 3 describes the Single School Planning process, outlined here:

1. Assess needs from multiple sources

2. Create a Single School Plan

3. Gather formative data from multiple sources

4. Reflect on information

5. Revise/modify implementation, as needed

6. Perform a summative assessment

What about people who refuse to participate or who sabotage the process?

As noted in the decision points within the LOU process (Figure 2.2), each individual decides whether he or she will move on to the next level. That is an internal decision. Some people may go through the motions to satisfy directives or expectations of administrators, but may actively demonstrate use only when being observed. For these resistant individuals, there are strategies to help support the effort:

- Listen to their concerns and objections to identify any real issues that need to be addressed. You may want to have this initial discussion in a one-on-one conversation, rather than a full group, to gather a better understanding of the issues in a neutral environment.
- Invite representative resistant teachers to participate on your planning and implementation teams. Their input is vital and ensures that all perspectives are considered. However, these individuals should not be allowed to circumvent the process.
- Ensure all stakeholders have the information they need about the innovation. This can be accomplished through information meetings, site inservices, staff meeting updates and table group

conversations, department meeting agendas or discussions, articles, and parent meetings.

- Provide opportunities for the teachers to observe other teachers throughout the district who are effectively using the innovation within their own content area.
- Provide peer-coaching support from credible colleagues, if appropriate.
- Put 90 percent of your efforts toward those individuals who are willing to actively participate in the process.

Case Studies

The following case studies illustrate how two principals address change at their site in the implementation of reform efforts. The first case demonstrates how a high school principal systematically incorporates strategies using the CBAM model. The second case study illustrates a more conventional approach to implementing mandated reforms.

 Case Study 1: Incorporating CBAM Reform Strategies and Change Principles

Municipal High School

As the school year began, Anna S., a second-year principal at Municipal High School, was prepared to meet the challenge of addressing the converging district and state mandates to improve student test scores, ensure all students graduate from high school, improve student attendance, and maintain a safe and orderly environment. Anna had a clear vision for school improvement and knew that this would require some major changes in the culture, structure, and practices of the school. Recognizing the implications of the change process on individuals within the organization, she held a series of special staff meetings in the final months of the previous school year. During these meetings, Anna addressed the following:

- Specific goals based upon multiple assessment measures
- Key points about the change process
- The administration of the "Self Assessment of Implementation" of the National Staff Development Council's (NSDC) Standards, as a needs assessment

Because she was knowledgeable about the change process, Anna was not concerned with the predictable reluctance of some staff members to engage in the process. She and her administrative team made a point of walking around, talking informally to each teacher about the process, and listening carefully to his or her concerns and comments. Anna's team factored these concerns into the professional development section of the Single School Plan. Staff meetings throughout the year were structured to provide time for teachers in small groups to share problems and successes in implementing the new practices they targeted.

The Instructional Leadership Team, which included representation from each department, classified staff, students, and parents, developed a comprehensive Single School Plan based upon the identified goals and assessed needs of the school, with an embedded professional development plan that reflected best practices and acknowledged the highly individualized nature of professional development as a tool in changing practice. The Single School Plan reflected continuous progress assessments throughout the year, with opportunities for modifications or adjustments, as needed.

Anna also ensured that her co-administrators thoroughly understood the change process and its implications by including the topic for discussion at administrative staff meetings. All administrators included considerations about change and adult learning theory in their teacher evaluation observations and conversations.

As part of the assessment process, Anna and her co-administrators continued to engage in discussions with individual teachers on an informal (conversations in the halls, lunch rooms, staff work room, etc.) and formal (teacher evaluation goal-setting, progress, and end-of-year evaluation meetings) basis about how they were progressing in implementing some of the key innovations that were included in the Single School Plan. All staff members, including Anna and her administrative team, were required to develop an Individual Professional Development Plan and participate in goal-setting meetings with a peer coach or administrator at the beginning of the year, regardless of whether or not they were scheduled for a contractual formal performance evaluation.

Anna and the School Leadership Team (SLT) also conducted an in-depth assessment of available resources. Anna shared the information about the school's funding resources, including the school's discretionary budget allocation, as well as categorical funds restricted for use with targeted populations or areas. The SLT also brainstormed a list of effective professional developers/trainers within the school, the district, the County Office of Education, the State Department of

Education, and local universities. The SLT utilized this information in determining funding and resources for specific areas of the Single School Plan.

Points to Consider

- Create a clear vision that describes what your school will look like when every child is achieving his or her full academic and social potential. Articulate this vision to your staff, students, and community often! (See Chapter 1, School Culture, and Chapter 3, The Single School Plan)
- Provide opportunities for each stakeholder to envision his or her role in the reform effort.
- Learn, integrate, and apply the Stages of Concern (SOC) and Levels of Use (LOU) information into your decision making. Understanding where people are in the process, why they do what they do, and how to provide appropriate support is crucial.
- Practice assessing where people are in the change process by asking the right questions and, most importantly, listening to their responses.
- The Single School Plan should reflect an understanding of the time required to move the organization through the change process. Remember, it takes 3 to 5 years (or more) to fully institutionalize change.
- Develop (with stakeholder input) a comprehensive professional development plan based on the assessed needs of staff to meet the school goals and objectives. Include multiple levels of training and support that specifically address identified Levels of Use (LOU).
- Establish a baseline for implementation of the changes you are planning to undertake. This will allow you to more effectively assess progress.
- Provide appropriate support to staff in the form of time, materials, opportunities for professional development, and coaching support. Build these support mechanisms into your Single School Plan.
- As your school progresses through the change process each year, don't forget that new staff may be back at the Non-Use and Awareness stages. Build opportunities to move them forward. This can be done through workshops, department meeting updates, mentor support, peer coaching, and providing needed materials.

- Include representation from the "naysayers" on the various decision-making committees. They will bring up the hard questions and issues that need to be addressed.
- Recognize and reward those individuals who take the risk to learn new skills and knowledge. Continue to encourage non-participating staff to participate in the process and offer incentives to do so.
- Block out dedicated time each day to do 5-minute drop-in visits to classrooms to see what is actually happening.
- Talk to staff frequently and individually about what and how they are doing. It shows you care. It also provides valuable data in the formative assessment of your Single School Plan.
- Don't forget that you, as the principal or co-administrator, are also going through the same process as you learn and implement the skills necessary to provide effective leadership. Letting staff know that you are a co-learner in the process heightens your credibility.

 ## Case Study 2: Incorporating Conventional Reform Strategies

Greenview Middle School

For the past three years, Mary M. has been a co-administrator at Greenview Middle School. Beginning her first year as principal, she was frustrated by the constant and conflicting demands of the state and the district administration regarding improving student test scores, ensuring all students are prepared to move up to the high school, improving student and teacher attendance, and maintaining a safe and orderly environment. Over the summer, she spent many hours at home developing the Single School Plan, with identified goals in each area for the upcoming school year. She also arranged for some national staff development presenters to conduct three workshops throughout the year: one on assessment, one on cooperative learning, and one on classroom management. She didn't have the funds available to do any additional professional development activities since each of the presenters charged so much money that it took up the entire professional development allocation in her budget.

During the opening staff meeting, Mary presented the Single School Plan. She was dismayed to hear moans and critical comments, but knew that those people probably wouldn't participate anyway and so she wrote them off. Four teachers volunteered to work on implementing the Single School Plan. An initial meeting was held to discuss the plan, with a follow-up meeting in March to discuss progress. No assessment data was provided, but the discussion was cordial.

Her co-administrators required that each teacher attend the scheduled professional development workshops. Throughout the year they observed teachers one or two times but provided no feedback other than the required teacher evaluation forms, which were left in their boxes. Pre- and post-conferences were not held since they were so busy with student discipline. As a result of the failure of the school to address the change process, twelve teachers were put on directed assistance when administrators observed them struggling to successfully implement some cooperative learning strategies. Six teachers applied for transfers during the course of the year.

Points to Consider

- Without a clear vision for school improvement, efforts will be disjointed, ineffective, and sporadic.
- Remember: One size does not fit all. Don't fall into the trap of a one-dimensional Single School Plan without considering the different Levels of Use (LOU) and/or emotional buy-in from your staff.
- Don't try to develop plans or implement change without including key stakeholders in the process.
- Be cautious about taking punitive actions on staff at the Mechanical stage (Figure 2.2). Learning a new skill involves the risk of failure.
- You cannot force someone to move from the Orientation and Preparation stages into actual use. Neither can you force anyone to move beyond the Routine use (Figure 2.2). That is an individual decision.
- It is easy to fill up all your time with administrative distractions such as student discipline and parent phone calls. Effective administrators collaborate together to block out sanctioned time for classroom observations, pre- and post-conferences, and general discussion with individual staff members to provide ongoing support as they progress through the change process.

Summary

Being the principal of a secondary school is a challenging position. For those principals and other instructional leaders faced with the task of improving student performance through specific reform efforts, the challenge is even greater.

Any administrator who is going through a school reform effort will benefit from knowing about and applying the wide range of rich information found in the change literature. Changing the culture of a school to reflect a vision of ongoing student improvement is a complex, time-consuming, and personal process for every stakeholder. Principals and instructional leaders should consider the process of change itself—the phases that each individual goes through as he or she progresses—and provide an environment that encourages and supports the learning of new behaviors and strategies, risk taking in implementing new learning, collaboration in problem solving and decision making, and the values and norms of a learning community dedicated to the vision of improving the achievement of all students.

Application Activity

1. Identify actions taken by each of the case study principals that were impacted by the "principles of change" and the CBAM model. How were the actions impacted?

2. What is your school's vision?

3. Who are the key stakeholder groups within your organization?

4. What resources (funding, people, time) are available to provide support?

5. What stakeholder representatives will you include in the planning and implementation process?

6. How will you assess the stakeholders' readiness based on the LOU/SOC process?

7. What specific support mechanisms are already in place to support each stage of the LOU and SOC? What additional support mechanisms might be needed?

8. Who are the "innovators" on campus who can provide support and leadership to staff?

3

The Single School Plan

Do We Have Consensus? Are We There Yet?

Bottom line: Schools must have a Single School Plan if the district/school receives federal funds. Effective school leaders have heeded the requirement for the creation of a multifaceted Single School Plan that identifies funding sources and outlines school goals, measurable objectives, related activities, responsible parties, timelines, evidence, and resources, both human and financial. The ultimate goal of a Single School Plan is to identify strategies to improve student achievement in a safe and orderly environment conducive to learning.

Past practice at many schools involved the development of a variety of individual action plans with a specific focus, such as professional development or school safety. Frequently, the authors of the action plans did not collaborate, thereby duplicating activities and resources. Too often, these plans ended up gathering dust on a bookshelf. An effective strategy for implementing secondary school reform is the creation of a Single School Plan (SSP).

The development, implementation, ongoing monitoring and assessment, as well as the revision processes of a Single School Plan require organization and persistence on the part of the school leadership. The Single School Plan can ultimately provide direction to stakeholders in improving the academic achievement of all students using one document.

Preparing a Single School Plan: The Beginning

The preparation of a Single School Plan may appear to be a daunting assignment the first time a school leader attempts the task. Consider these five steps to begin the development of a Single School Plan:

1. **Identify a Single School Plan team.** This team may consist of the School Site Council or an ad hoc task force. Effective school leaders seek individuals from all stakeholder groups, including parents and community members, who enjoy organizing, planning, and attending to details, to be a part of the planning team.

2. **Set meeting dates and a timeline for completion of the Single School Plan.** Once the planning team has been identified, the next task is to find time to bring the committee together to create a Single School Plan to improve student achievement. Although the principal initiates the first meeting, the committee may develop the subsequent meeting dates and timeline for completion.

3. **Establish meeting norms.** Collaboratively set boundaries for the planning conversations. Plan for how to address areas of disagreement.

4. **Frontload the process!** Provide sufficient information, including legislative mandates, disaggregated student performance data, and other relevant data, to establish the focus and direction for the planning process.

5. **Review the school's vision and mission statement.**

Vision and the Single School Plan

What does a school vision statement have to do with the Single School Plan? The Single School Plan adds flesh to the skeletal structure of the school's vision statement. Before an effective Single School Plan can be developed, the school must have a clear vision of what student performance will look like in the future. Today, a school vision for students may look like a narrative statement or a list of expected outcomes such as this: effective communicator, life-long learner, critical thinker and problem solver, contributing citizen, and so on.

Vision clarifies the direction of the organization. It is shaped by the school's culture. A vision is multifaceted. It is future-oriented, results-oriented, proactive, and motivational. The vision establishes clear standards of excellence for all students; it is feasible; and it should be communicated and translated to all stakeholders in the educational community. The vision reflects a shared dream and the desired results for student learning in all stakeholder groups.

The Mission Statement

Once a shared vision is created, representatives from all stake-holder groups collaboratively create the mission statement prior to the development of the school's Single School Plan. The mission statement conveys the identity and purpose of the school. It puts into words why the school exists. Mission statements generally reflect a five-year forecast. The Cambridge Group (2003) identifies three elements to include in a mission statement:

- **Identity** describes the unique qualities of the organization.
- **Purpose** describes the desired result of the organization.
- **Means** describes how the organization will achieve its purpose.

Putting all of these elements together, a sample school mission statement might look like this:

"The mission of _____ school, an enriched learning network (identity), is to ensure that all students master rigorous academic learning standards and become productive, socially responsible citizens (purpose), through a commitment to excellence supported by highly trained and qualified staff and vital community partnerships (means)."

Consider Elements of Culture, Planning, and Accountability

Myths, Legends, and Critical Issues

A clear vision and purposeful mission statement support learning communities as they move through the reform process. A learning community is a group of people with a shared interest in the knowledge, application, and improvement of professional educational standards (see Chapter 5). Awareness of the myths, legends (see Chapter 1), and critical issues affects the school's ability to assess and evaluate student academic performance and the teaching and learning process. It also supports the ability of a learning community to problem solve.

Critical issues are defined as issues that must be systematically addressed if the organization is to survive or to recreate itself in the context of its own stated mission (The Cambridge Group, 2003).

The Status Quo

Successful learning communities are aware of past and present demographic and academic trends as well as myths and legends about the school. Before a Single School Plan is developed, it is important to take some time to gather information about "how we do things around here" by listening to the stories of the school's past (see Chapter 1). Assessments will tell you the *current* academic and social *perceptions* about the school. Taking time to research the school's past performance and listen to staff, parents, and community leaders will flesh out and give more texture to the "status quo."

Identify Accountability Obligations

Awareness of the status quo provides school leaders with a better understanding of what assessment tools to use in gathering data for the purpose of evaluation. Accountability involves the external obligation for evaluation evidence (Guskey, 2000). School accountability report cards are one example of external obligations. Various legislative mandates, such as the federal priorities identified in the *No Child Left Behind Act* of 2001 (NCLB), state education codes, local district and school priorities, as well as grant and other funding source requirements, identify external obligations. Even more importantly, parents and community members hold school leaders accountable for the academic performance of all students. Consequently, the Single School Plan is a primary accountability tool for secondary school leaders involved in the implementation of state and federal mandates.

Preparing a Single School Plan: The Writing

Be Strategic

Strategic planning implies that the goals and tasks identified in the Single School Plan are thoughtful, intentional, and deliberate. The plan identifies specific tasks that will move the school from the status quo to an improved position. A strategic Single School Plan is intentionally aligned with the vision of the school district. Short-term goals and benchmarks are deliberately included in a Single School Plan so that the school community stays focused on the ultimate goal of improving student achievement.

A Single School Plan documents how a school will achieve goals based on the school's vision and mission through a series of prioritized tasks and within the given constraints of the school or district. A Single School Plan addresses how a school will improve the status quo in relation to the goal(s) of the school mission statement. The plan does not address day-to-day operations unless they specifically relate to actions necessary to move the reform agenda forward. The school's vision is the key component of a successful, strategic Single School Plan.

Qualities of a Strategic Single School Plan (SSP)

- The SSP is aligned with the district goals and priorities.
- The SSP is aligned with the school's vision and mission.
- The SSP focuses on critical issues.
- The SSP is student results-oriented.
- The SSP reflects the integration of the professional development plan and other related school improvement plans (e.g., Safety Plan).

When these five qualities are incorporated, the document becomes a valuable resource for school leaders. Principals should always use the goals from the school's plan to support staffing needs, budget requests, professional development activities, and community partnership projects.

Creating a Single School Plan is not a task; it is a process that produces a product. Successful learning communities develop, implement, monitor, assess, and modify the comprehensive Single School Plan at various intervals along the reform process, based on identified needs from all stakeholder groups and additional student achievement data.

Six Components of a Single School Plan

The following chart (Figure 3.1) illustrates the essential components of a Single School Plan. These components build upon each other. Notice how the school's vision is transparent throughout the development of the Single School Plan. The school's vision must clearly state the direction of the organization. The vision and mission statements are developed as a result of a consensus-building process involving professional staff, district personnel, the community, parents, and business and industry representatives. If any component is missing, the Single School Plan becomes another dusty document sitting on the bookshelf in the principal's office.

The Six Components of a Single School Plan are

1. Expected student outcomes

2. Goals and short-range (1–2 years) objectives for each goal

3. Specific tasks and intervention strategies to address the objectives (includes timelines, resources, and persons responsible)

4. Assessment indicators (with formative benchmarks and summative evidence)

5. Communication mechanisms

6. Procedures for reflection, analysis, and modification of Single School Plan

Expected Student Outcomes

The term or phrase a school uses to describe the shared vision and the definition of the desired results for student learning may vary.

Figure 3.1   Essential Components of a Single School Plan

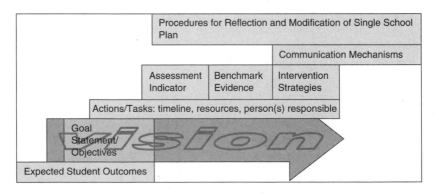

Some schools refer to these outcomes as "Expected Schoolwide Learning Results," or "Desired Results for Student Learning," or "Expected Student Outcomes." No matter which phrase a school uses, it is important that the performance indicators that define the learning outcomes are developed by a group of people who represent both the school and the community.

The National Study of School Evaluation outlines a process used to identify and develop the expected student outcomes in their planning guide, *School Improvement: Focusing on Student Performance* (Fitzpatrick, 1997). State Consolidated Plans also address the need for identification of expected student outcomes.

A typical process includes the following steps:

1. Review the school's mission statement.

2. Review the school community's belief about student learning.

3. Review current educational research and literature on maximizing student learning.

4. Review current school, district, state, and national standards and benchmarks for student learning.

5. Develop an initial draft of common expectations for student academic achievement.

6. Analyze current district and school student performance data.

7. Define the desired results for student learning.

Identify Goals and Objectives

The overarching purpose of the Single School Plan is to accomplish the desired student learning outcomes. Matching up the past academic trends, present achievement data, and future goals will identify "the gap" between the status quo and the desired outcome stated in the mission statement. The goals in the Single School Plan will provide a roadmap for a school to close "the gap." Three to five broad-based goals are a reasonable number to find in a Single School Plan.

Specific, measurable objectives should be developed for each goal statement. Objectives outline how each goal will be accomplished, much as a lesson objective specifies what students will know and be able to do. Typically, there are three to five objectives for each goal. Assessment data should directly reflect evidence that demonstrates how each objective is met.

The *No Child Left Behind Act* of 2001 (NCLB)

The *No Child Left Behind Act* of 2001 was signed into law on January 8, 2002 (PL107-110). The legislation set out key performance goals for all states to close the achievement gap with accountability, flexibility, and choice, so that no child is left behind. Among those goals are the following:

1. All students will be taught by highly qualified teachers* by the end of the 2005–2006 school year. (Title I, Part A, Section 1119 (a) (2))

2. All English learners will master English and meet the same rigorous standards for academic achievement. (Title III, Part B, Section 3202)

3. All students will learn in schools that are safe and drug free. (Title IV, Part A, Section 4002)

---

*The *No Child Left Behind Act* of 2001 requires that each state develop a plan identifying how schools will meet the requirements of the federal legislation. In California, the state plan requires that teachers have a bachelor's degree, have state certification, and demonstrate subject-area knowledge for each core subject they teach in order to meet the "highly qualified" performance goal. (California Department of Education, 2004).

As the reader can see, words such as "proficiency," "demonstrate," "highly qualified," and "safe and drug free" are deliberately vague in order to give state legislators, school boards, and administrators latitude to make interpretations that will fit local needs. Be sure to check with your Human Resources Department, Educational Services Department, and State Department of Education's Web site to obtain local definitions and performance indicators for each of the goals set forth by NCLB.

Adequate Yearly Progress (AYP)

In addition to federally identified performance goals, school leaders must also meet state accountability goals. Each state is required to develop and implement a statewide accountability system that will ensure all schools and districts meet "Adequate Yearly Progress (AYP)" in language arts and mathematics as defined by NCLB. Some states have expanded the accountability systems to include achievement goals in all core content areas.

According to the U.S. Department of Education, this accountability system for each state must be based on academic standards and assessments. It must include a process to ensure the achievement of state academic standards by all students. In addition, it must include sanctions and rewards to hold all public schools accountable for improving student achievement. State departments of education offer a variety of resources online to assist school leaders as they develop a Single School Plan to document how a school will ensure all students meet the Adequate Yearly Progress goals.

Tasks

Single School Plan tasks are strategic and sequential activities that are measurable and take place over time to meet the desired goals. A clear, challenging, and practical set of tasks is more likely to be completed than vague, unrealistic, "pie-in-the-sky" activities that are written to satisfy legislative mandates. Practical tasks, with clear benchmark evidence, bring learning communities together because the tasks provide opportunities for people to actively participate in moving the reform agenda forward. "Pie-in-the-sky" activities reinforce the common perception that a Single School Plan is nothing but a political document developed by the principal, or designee, to meet mandate requirements.

Assessment Indicators, Benchmarks, and Timelines

The fourth component of the Single School Plan targets specific assessment indicators used to determine success in meeting each goal's objectives. These indicators identify sources and types of evidence to collect to determine progress. The Single School Plan should list only those assessment indicators that pertain to the specific goals. Some data sources may be used as evidence for multiple objectives.

Clearly written *benchmarks* will identify the evidence that demonstrates progress toward achievement of tasks. It is a good idea to notify the educational community when benchmark activities are met. A *timeline* for accomplishing goals, especially during the early stages of implementation, will help a school staff stay focused. Throughout a typical rapid-fire day, the secondary school administrator might be dealing with athletic emergencies, multiple student assemblies, finding classroom coverage due to lack of substitutes, student relationship crises, school toilets overflowing, an extremely angry and vocal parent demanding that the administrator dismiss a particular teacher immediately, following up on a rumor about a drug deal taking place behind the handball courts, and an unscheduled drop-in visit by one of the school board members. Very few school leaders can juggle Single School Plan deadlines and deal with crises simultaneously without the aid of a timeline listing specific activities to help them stay focused.

Communication Mechanisms

The listing of communication mechanisms in the Single School Plan is an often-overlooked section. It is important for school leaders to apprise all stakeholders of the progress the school is making toward the completion of each task on a regular basis. Make use of newsletters; e-mail updates; school Web sites; and annual reports to community groups, students, and staff to keep everyone informed and involved in the goal of improving student achievement.

Procedures for Reflection, Analysis, and Modification of Single School Plan

Include procedures and timelines in your school calendar for reflection, analysis of new student performance data, and updating and modifying the Single School Plan. Consider adding a section to your faculty meeting agenda template for revisiting the goals of the Single School Plan at least three times a year.

Putting the Pieces Together

1. Put your planning team, process, and timeline in place.

2. Revisit the school's vision and mission with the entire staff through the lens of the mandate to leave no child behind. Do not dwell on this process to the detriment of moving forward to create a Single School Plan.

3. Create a plan to achieve the vision.

4. Identify time on the school calendar to monitor, review, and update the Single School Plan throughout the year.

5. Gather data from multiple data sources to accumulate information over a period of time.

6. Reflect on the information: What is working? What is not? What needs to be changed or modified?

7. Revise and modify implementation as necessary. Make changes, as needed, to the Single School Plan based on new assessment data.

8. Keep a log of strategies that worked and ideas to consider the following year.

9. *Communicate, communicate, communicate* with stakeholders throughout the process.

The following template (Figure 3.2) is just one example of how you might format your Single School Plan.

Figure 3.2 Sample Single School Plan Template

Goal 1:							
Objective	Task	Person Responsible	Timeline	Resources Available	Resources Needed	Benchmark Evidence	Reporting Method(s)
1.							
2.							
3.							

Case Studies

The following case studies illustrate how two principals approach the development of the Single School Plan to improve student achievement and strengthen learning communities. The first case reveals how a principal builds on current staff expertise and prior momentum to fulfill a district mandate. The second case study reveals how important it is for school leaders to be observant and adaptable during the Single School Planning process.

Case Study 1: Capitalizing on Staff Expertise and Prior Momentum

Birch Knoll High School

The previous principal at Birch Knoll High School accepted an early retirement package the district offered to employees last May after the school moved into Program Improvement, Year 3 status. Carl A. was thrilled to be appointed principal in August. As a co-administrator at Birch Knoll High School the past three years, Carl had been assigned to work with a variety of staff and community groups. However, the previous principal did not include Carl or the other co-administrators in very many instructional projects. Nevertheless, Carl is familiar with many of the teachers and community leaders. Carl is also aware of the few disgruntled staff members who usually sabotage any efforts to change the status quo.

During the second week of school, Principal Carl A. received a memorandum from the superintendent's office outlining the documents each school needed to submit during the first quarter of school. Among those documents was the updated Single School Plan.

Carl is aware that the student subgroups that did not meet the AYP criteria are the students enrolled in special education classes and students designated Limited English Proficient (LEP). Although 95 percent of the students were tested the previous year, Carl understands that if the school does not meet the AYP criteria this year for all student subgroups, the school may face sanctions from the state Title I office.

Carl prepared a memorandum for the returning members of the safe school committee, the parent-teacher association, and the faculty advisory committee, inviting them to appoint a representative to attend a planning meeting of the School Site Council the following week. Carl included information about the external facilitator along with the school's current school plan; an agenda for the first meeting; and a tentative calendar of subsequent meeting dates, times, and locations.

Carl met the next day with the five staff leaders involved in the previous year's planning meetings to develop the Single School Plan, and asked them to participate in the upcoming meeting. Two respectfully declined, citing lack of time due to their increased workload. One teacher reminded Carl that he would be retiring at the end of the semester and also declined. The remaining two veteran teachers were highly respected by staff and thoroughly understood the culture of the school. Carl was able to recruit a new English Language Development teacher and a special education teacher to participate on the Single School Plan committee.

Carl contacted the district's categorical director and asked him to attend the afterschool planning meeting the following week. He asked him to "lay the foundation" for the Single School Plan by explaining the requirements of the *No Child Left Behind Act* of 2001, as well as the AYP criteria and sanctions.

Carl was pleased with the results of the meeting the following week; however, he wished he had scheduled more time for discussion. The Single School Plan committee met the following month and reviewed the most current student achievement data, and identified the gap between the current student achievement levels and the AYP targets for each subgroup. The committee formed into teams. Each team was assigned one subgroup, analyzed that subgroup's disaggregated data, and developed recommendations for specific strategies and interventions to improve student achievement. These recommendations were presented to the entire committee at the next meeting.

At the end of six weeks, the planning committee members completed an initial draft of the Single School Plan and presented their findings to the entire faculty. Carl submitted the draft Single School Plan to the superintendent at the end of November.

Points to Consider

- Include both new and veteran staff members on your Single School Plan team.
- Parent participation is mandatory under NCLB guidelines. Include parent and faculty representatives from each of the student subgroups, including socioeconomically disadvantaged, English Learner, and special education students.

- Schedule sufficient time for the committee members to review and discuss the outcome of the previous planning process.
- Recruit Single School Plan committee members early. Be sure they understand and commit to the time requirements of the process.
- Using categorical funds, a school can hire external evaluators to conduct the actual data analysis for the school's Single School Plan and write the end-of-the-year data analysis report.
- Many businesses and community-based organizations have personnel trained in strategic planning and organizational development. Invite them to assist.
- Include representatives from all stakeholder groups on your planning team.
- Be clear about the purpose of a Single School Plan.
- It is essential to regularly revisit and modify the plan based on formative and summative data.

RVMS   Case Study 2: Observing and Adapting in the Planning Process

Ridge View Middle School

Principal Tony R. has just completed his second year at Ridge View Middle School. Prior to becoming a principal, Tony was a co-administrator for five years at a high school and served on the district strategic planning team.

There are 45 teachers at Ridge View Middle School. Ten percent of the students are enrolled in special education classes and 35 percent of the students are designated Limited English Proficient (LEP). The school is starting its third year as a Program Improvement school.

Tony was eager to begin the planning process for the Single School Plan during the summer. The previous year, Tony had introduced the concept of using a variety of assessment measures to assess student progress. In addition, the Ridge View Middle School staff had conducted an analysis of student work and determined that many of the special education and LEP students were not keeping up with the learning pace identified by the district office.

Tony identified five staff members he felt would represent the "voice" of the faculty to be on the Single School Plan committee. Next, he contacted the PTA president and asked for three volunteers to represent parents and the community. Tony began planning meetings to revise the Single School Plan in August and presented the updated Single School Plan to the faculty in September.

The Ridge View Middle School staff listened patiently to the updated Single School Plan. Tony pointed out that assessment evidence would be gathered throughout the year to determine student progress. During the last five minutes of the meeting, one teacher asked if the same evidence could be used against a teacher during the evaluation process. Another pointed out that the updated Single School Plan goals were similar to the ones used four years ago when the original Single School Plan was developed by the previous principal. A third teacher asked who would be analyzing the evidence to determine student progress.

As the teachers left the meeting, Tony overheard comments such as, "It's a good thing we work at a middle school because we can just send these kids on to the high school." "Another year, another plan." "If we wait long enough, this too shall pass." "So what are they really going to do to us if we don't follow this plan?"

The next day, Tony spoke individually with teachers during passing periods about concerns raised at the meeting. Individually, the teachers shared their frustration that Tony had fallen victim to the same administrative malady as the previous principal. Everyone agreed that the tasks identified in the Single School Plan were thoughtful and appeared to solve the dilemma of poor student performance. The problem was that the Single School Plan did not reflect the needs of the students and staff at Ridge View Middle School.

Tony went back to his office to make a few notes to remind himself to revisit the Single School Plan in a month, after he gathered more information. He realized he knew a lot about the Single School Planning process, but may have needed to provide more opportunities for staff members to give input during that process.

Points to Consider

- Planning and developing a successful Single School Plan takes time and requires participation by community leaders, parents, staff, teachers, and students. The planning process can provide an opportunity to build community. It will probably unearth underlying cultural beliefs that may have prevented reform progress in the past.
- Someone outside of your organization might best facilitate the initial meetings. It is very difficult to participate as a member of the team and facilitate the meeting at the same time.

- It is important to gather input from a variety of stakeholder groups. However, the planning team should not try to do a "group write" of the actual plan. Identify one or two people to do the actual writing based upon the input from the group. Present the draft document to the planning team for review and revision, as needed, at the next team meeting.
- Be sure to consider the teachers' contract. Be clear about how observational and student work evidence collected for the Single School Plan will be used. Lack of clarity results in distrust between staff and administration.

Summary

This chapter introduced the physical representation of a school's vision: the Single School Plan. This plan integrates all other school-related plans, such as the professional development plan and the school safety plan, into a cohesive, coordinated Single School Plan. This chapter outlined specific steps, tips, and cautions to consider in the planning process. The planning document should clearly stipulate overarching goals that address the vision, as well as school and district priorities; specific, measurable objectives; tasks to accomplish each objective; a timeline; designated person responsible; funding sources; data/evidence; and communication to stakeholders. As described in this chapter, the Single School Plan is strategic, student results-oriented, and provides a clear map for all.

Application Activity

1. Who are some of the key stakeholders at your school?

2. What are some available data sources?

3. What are the shared beliefs (convictions) and values about education among the stakeholders?

4. How do the school vision and mission support the shared beliefs and values of the group? Do they need to be modified?

5. What do current student performance and accountability data say about your school?

6. What are the current self-imposed limits or constraints of your school? (Policies, organizational structures, decision-making process, etc.)

7. How does the school's culture impact operational decisions: budgetary reality, faculty and staff capabilities and needs, facilities, ability to assess student learning and achievement, ability to collect and analyze student performance data, other resource needs and availability?

8. What are the school's areas of strength?

9. What are the school's areas for growth?

10. What school artifacts demonstrate that reflection, analysis, and modification procedures and activities are used at your school to implement school reform?

PART II

Shared Decision Making

4

Professional Development

It's Not Fluff!

Professional development in the American educational system has typically consisted of fragmented, disconnected, one-shot "sit 'n' git" workshops on topics selected by the principal or district office personnel as necessary for teachers and administrators. Sound familiar? The workshops may or may not be considered valuable or necessary to the staff members themselves, and, in fact, are often perceived as boring and a waste of time. Even if they are perceived as interesting or important, there is often little in the way of two-way conversations, follow-up, or actual implementation of the content into classroom practice. Quite often, these workshops reflect the mandates of various pieces of legislation, grants, or district goals, and may or may not reflect the goals outlined in the school plan.

This chapter will review the descriptors of effective professional development; examine research on best practices in the field; and provide suggestions for the process of developing, implementing, and evaluating an effective secondary staff development plan.

What Is Professional Development?

Thomas Guskey (2000, p. 16) defines professional development as "those processes and activities designed to enhance the professional knowledge, skills, and attitudes of educators so that they might, in turn, improve the learning of students." The focus is on improving student achievement. The design for using professional development activities begins with identifying what each individual within the system should know and be able to do to achieve the goals set by the organization.

Although designed with the best of intentions, most workshops offered in the old staff development model have proven to be ineffective. In conducting research into the impact of existing staff development offerings, Bruce Joyce and Beverly Showers (2000) produced some rather startling findings:

- After a presentation of theory or information, only 5 percent of learners actually transferred that information into practice.
- A combination of the presentation of information and a demonstration of skills/knowledge resulted in a 10 percent transfer into practice.
- Combining the presentation of information, a demonstration, and an opportunity to practice the new learning resulted in a 20 percent transfer into practice.
- Combining the presentation, demonstration, and practice with feedback resulted in 25 percent of transfer into practice.
- Combining the presentation, demonstration, practice, and feedback *with ongoing coaching* resulted in 90 percent of transfer into practice!

But even this information is insufficient when considering how to construct a highly effective professional development program. Have you ever been to workshops where some participants are reading the newspaper in the back of the room and others are correcting papers, knitting, balancing their checkbooks, or just making jokes throughout the presentation? Adults learn and apply new information on a "need to know" basis. If they see no connection between the information and their work, they do not perceive a need to know. A critical role of the school principal is to provide sufficient data, information, and incentive to develop this "need to know" attribute among staff members, and to provide appropriate professional development opportunities and support for staff.

Elements of Professional Development

The National Staff Development Council and various task force committees across the United States have examined at length the question,

"What are the design elements of high-quality staff development?" These identified elements should be carefully considered by those engaged in planning an effective, high-quality professional development program at the site or district level. The following 10 elements, outlined in the *California Field Guide for Teachers' Professional Development*, summarize the best thinking to date about this critical area:

1. Student Data: We begin with disaggregated schoolwide and individual student data (by race, ethnicity, gender, grade level, and NCLB subgroups). It is important that the entire staff examines multiple data sources throughout the year, rather than focus only on a review of standardized test scores each fall. This data should include results on state achievement tests, benchmark assessments in the core area, individual teacher assessment data, and any other data that will provide greater clarity on how well students are learning the content and identify those who are not.

2. Professional Development Plan: High-quality professional development should address the goals of the district and the school, as well as the needs of individuals within the school. In addressing the learning goals of all students, the plan should therefore be developed in alignment with the development, monitoring, and evaluation of the Single School Plan. During the planning and monitoring phases, the following areas should be considered: standards and curriculum; strategies to address the needs of English Learners, special education, and low socioeconomic students; analyzing assessment data; gaining an understanding of the diverse cultural, racial, and ethnic backgrounds of students; and educating parents to partner with the school.

3. Time for Professional Development: Many states provide 2 to 5 days during the school year for professional development. However, professional development is most effective when it is job-embedded so that new learning can be utilized and practiced on a daily basis. For systemic growth to occur, sanctioned time should be made available, weekly and monthly, throughout the year for staff to engage in professional conversations around classroom practice. (Yes, that's professional development, too!) Rather than wait for additional professional development days to be added onto the school year, it is necessary to carefully examine what time may be available within the current calendar and daily schedules. The following table outlines a variety of ways to find the time needed to provide a comprehensive and coherent professional development program.

Figure 4.1   Finding Time for Professional Development

Option	Comments
Purchase time Release days Summer or Saturday stipends Added days to the contract	These are usually "one-shot" options rather than ongoing activities. Expenses can be prohibitive. All teachers may not want to participate in the summer or Saturday option.
Reallocate or "free up" time Expand staffing Substitute pool Part-time teachers Retired teachers	Providing qualified substitutes will ease concerns about teachers' absences from the classroom, but almost always costs money.
Flexible coverage Classroom coverage by teaching assistants, college interns, other teachers, administrators Informal (occasional) team teaching During special events or schoolwide activities (such as assemblies)	These are relatively cost-free options, but are short-term, temporary strategies, which do not free up teachers for large periods of time and are sometimes resented by parents.
Alternative scheduling Common prep or planning time Formal team teaching (regular basis) Block scheduling Add extra period to master schedule Banking time (late arrival or early dismissal for students)	These strategies involve alteration of the calendar, school day, or teaching schedule (master schedule) on a long-term basis; they require careful planning, teacher participation, and administrative support. There may also be contractual issues regarding participation of teachers beyond the contracted workday that could result in additional costs.
Use existing time better Staff development days Faculty meetings Departmental meetings Grade-level meetings	

Reprinted, by permission, California Department of Education, CDE Press, 1430 N Street, Suite 3207, Sacramento, CA 95814.

4. Leadership: No principal or administrative team can create system-wide school reform without the support of teacher leaders. They may serve as pivotal members or leaders of key committees or provide professional development and coaching to staff members. Identify these people and ensure they have training opportunities to keep them up to date with curriculum, instruction, assessment, and facilitation skills.

5. Content and Pedagogy: The *No Child Left Behind Act* of 2001 has spotlighted the critical importance of having teachers who are expert in their content areas, as well as the pedagogy associated with that content area. In addition to subject-matter workshops and university coursework, principals should encourage opportunities for teachers to engage in in-depth, reflective problem-solving conversations that focus on improving the delivery of curriculum and instruction. This may be accomplished at department meetings, during peer-coaching reflective conversations, and in other venues that promote risk taking and honest self-assessment of pedagogy and lesson design.

6. Inquiry: In a school that emphasizes inquiry as a focus for professional development, teachers (and administrators) reflect on actions they have taken, think about the outcome of those actions, and plan for the "next time" or future application. The Plan, Teach (or act), Reflect, Apply model is the basis of the peer-coaching model used with beginning teachers and usually results in major growth on the part of individuals who genuinely engage in the process. Principal coaches are also being utilized in some districts to provide principals with a safe environment to reflect on school leadership issues and engage in planning and problem solving. Effective learning communities provide opportunities for faculty members to actively engage in discussions that allow them to reflect on their values and beliefs relative to student achievement, as well as opportunities to conduct and report action research. Collegial dialogues, around meeting the needs of all students, form the basis of administrative expectations. It is important that inquiry conversations and activities result in a product of some type, such as a department's agreement about content of lessons, minutes to a meeting, or a reflective log. Otherwise, conversations tend to lose focus and purpose (DuFour, 2003).

7. Collaboration: A large number of secondary schools might be characterized as culturally isolationist. Staff members often tend to value autonomy in the classroom and rarely collaborate in a meaningful way about the school's vision, goals, curriculum, pedagogy, or assessment data. This is in direct contrast to schools that value collective norms of behavior around collaboration in planning, goal setting, lesson plan development, problem solving, and student assessment monitoring for the purpose of improving student achievement. In collaborative secondary schools, administrators actively participate in and support professional development activities. Collaborative learning communities systematically design professional development activities that address the learning goals of each staff member to maximize student outcomes. Establishing a cultural norm of collaboration at a secondary school, particularly a school with long-standing traditions and beliefs, requires a major commitment and specific expectations by the principal for all stakeholders. As noted by Fullan (2003), what is required is actually "reculturing," and moving toward professional learning community culture. He further states that there is no model or template for how this may be accomplished. It must be developed and carried out within the context of each school. Principal leadership is crucial!

8. Adult Learning: Following the pioneering work of Malcolm Knowles, a great deal has been written over the past sixty years about how adults learn. Clearly, adults are influenced by a set of internal motivators that directly relate to a need to know. Many adults "check out" of professional development activities because they see no need for the information and cannot relate what is happening to their own professional lives. Some basic tenets of Adult Learning Theory to consider in planning professional development include the following:

1. The information should be job-embedded. Adults must be able to connect the content with what they need to know and be able to do as part of their day-to-day activities.

2. Adults need to have some control over the logistical details of their learning, including the content, the purpose, and the where, when, and how of the learning activities. In short, it is important to adult learners that they are treated as competent professionals, rather than being told what to do.

3. Adults will not attempt new learning if they perceive they will be made to look foolish or humiliated in any way. It is imperative to provide threat-free opportunities for adults to practice new skills, with support from peers.

4. Adults respond to nonjudgmental feedback from peers as they begin to apply new learning. Small-group activities that allow adults to discuss new learning with colleagues provide effective opportunities for adults to apply, analyze, synthesize, and evaluate new learning.

9. Support: It is impossible to provide a comprehensive and systematic professional development program without the support of the Board of Education, the superintendent, the district office, parents, and the community. The key to obtaining and maintaining a strong level of support for a comprehensive professional development program lies in communication: to what degree do you, as the principal, communicate the importance of your professional development activities based on research or data around student achievement? It is essential that the principal systematically include opportunities for representatives of all stakeholder groups to meet and discuss school issues and goals, including the professional development calendar for the year. You are talking to them about their students, their own children, their future employees, and the future leaders of the community. The more you communicate the goals of the school around improving the academic achievement of all students, the greater the support will be for your efforts to provide high-quality professional development.

10. Accountability: Within the educational arena, teachers and administrators are evaluated and held accountable for the achievement of all students through the legislated mandates of the *No Child Left Behind Act* of 2001. Professional development systems directly impact classroom interactions and the delivery of instruction. Therefore, it is essential to incorporate a process for collecting multiple professional development data sources, both formative and summative, which inform the actual effectiveness of professional development "offerings," and contribute to ongoing planning and revision. Examples of data might include formal and informal observational data, examples of student work, student benchmark data, lesson plans, professional development evaluations, reflection data, and surveys.

As the site principal, it is essential to provide teachers and instructional staff with timely and appropriate professional development and support throughout the journey of reform implementation. If school leaders do not address this critical need, any attempts to initiate reform efforts will result in burnout and/or passive resistance by teachers, and, eventually, the general breakdown of the entire process.

The process of planning and implementing a professional development plan may initially appear to be overwhelming. The following are some basic foundational steps that should be put into place that will support your efforts to put the pieces together:

- Ensure your professional development team is knowledgeable of Adult Learning Theory and the Change Process as a basis for creating the school's professional development plan.
- The Single School Plan goals and objectives provide the framework for planning professional development at the school.

Ensure that all stakeholders know what they are. Determine how you will communicate with them.

- With the planning team, identify the specific skills and knowledge that staff will need to put into practice to meet the school goals.
- After informing staff about the school goals and objectives, and the expectations for classroom practice, collect data from a Professional Development Needs Assessment that allows staff members to identify specific skills and knowledge needed to make the transition. (Caution: Many times, people "don't know what they don't know," and are unable to identify all the professional development components that they need.)
- The professional development team then designs a professional development plan that includes external (e.g., conferences, district/county workshops, etc.) and internal (e.g., school workshops, peer coaching, department meeting protocols) opportunities for staff to engage in meaningful, appropriate, and job-embedded professional development.

Case Studies

The following case studies illustrate how two principals approach the professional development needs of their staff. The first case study illustrates how a principal developed a multi-faceted professional development system that addressed the differentiated needs of staff. The second case study describes a typical disconnect between the school's professional development plan and the need of the faculty.

 Case Study 1: Differentiating Professional Development

Municipal High School

As part of the process of developing a Single School Plan, Anna's planning team first looked at each of the school's goals and determined to make all professional development decisions based on improving student achievement. They then examined research that outlined what worked and what didn't work in a secondary school setting, identifying specific skills, knowledge, and experiences needed by teachers, instructional staff, and parents to accomplish each of the school goals.

As a first step in developing a professional development plan that specifically addressed the Single School Plan, a needs assessment was filled out and submitted by every instructional staff member, including paraprofessionals. The needs assessment specified targeted skills and knowledge tied to school goals, rather than a menu of miscellaneous workshops. This data was thoroughly reviewed by the team and formed the basis for the professional development plan.

The plan integrated targeted workshops offered at the site and through the district office. It stipulated a bell schedule change to allow the school to bank minutes each week to provide 60 student-free minutes every other week for departments to collaborate, and it also set aside funds to buy period subs for teachers to enable them to conduct peer observations in each other's classrooms. Through the district's Human Resources Department, Anna collaborated with the bargaining unit for this schedule change since it resulted in a change in working conditions at the site.

The plan included a two-day staff retreat prior to the beginning of school to present the direction for the school year and provide time for the review of disaggregated student data and departmental planning. A full day at the end of the school year was calendared to review progress and begin planning for the next year. A calendar of 2-hour, topic-specific, afterschool workshops, Saturday workshops, and district workshops was made available to instructional staff. Site and district teachers, County Office of Education experts, and university partners provided these workshops. Every effort was made to ensure that these workshops were very high quality and had direct application to classroom practice. Anna and/or other site administrators attended and actively participated in each workshop. Workshop evaluations were reviewed and used in the decision-making process about future professional development offerings.

The school began to develop an on-site professional development library, with a wide range of current books, professional magazines, and videos that addressed each of the targeted goals. Instructional staff members were encouraged to check out the materials as resources to meet individual professional development goals.

Anna hired two full-time instructional coaches, one for mathematics and the other for language arts, from her Title I funds to provide ongoing coaching support and professional development, as well as facilitate ongoing content area/departmental professional conversations around data analysis, effective content-area pedagogy, and strategies for improving student achievement. The instructional coaches provided professional development to the faculty in the areas of reading, writing, and mathematics in the content areas. They were part of the school's leadership team and actively participated in the planning, implementation, and evaluation process targeting the school's identified goals and objectives. To maintain and improve their own skills and knowledge, instructional coaches attended district-level leadership meetings in their respective departments, attended conferences and advanced workshops in their content area, and participated in specific training to develop and enhance their coaching skills.

Anna hired two full-time roving substitute teachers, one of whom substituted on a period-by-period basis to allow all teachers to conduct peer observations. They also supported mentor teachers who had scheduled one to two periods for classroom observations and follow-up reflective conversations. Many classroom teachers voluntarily scheduled peer observations during their conference periods.

Anna and the planning team reviewed all school resources, including general fund and categorical budgets, human resources, and the school's calendar and bell schedule. Funding sources were identified and targeted for costs associated with workshop presentations, stipends, period and full-day subs, and professional development materials, as well as coaching support stipulated in the Single School Plan. Funds were also allocated for targeted university classes and a variety of online professional development opportunities. Anna reviewed the plan with the district educational services staff, who were able to provide additional funds through Title II and Title III to address professional development activities and materials that targeted beginning teachers and teachers of English Language Learners.

The professional development plan included a systematic process to evaluate its effectiveness over the course of the year. A comprehensive list of formal and informal formative and summative data sources, beginning with the needs assessment, and an implementation timeline were identified. Each staff member was expected to include individual professional development goals and objectives as part of the teacher goal-setting conference at the beginning of the school year. Teachers were encouraged to develop portfolios of their own best practices based on student data, reflective journals, and professional development logs. Data sources were reviewed at each leadership and planning team meeting, and modifications to the professional development plan were made, as needed.

Predictably, not every staff member at the school embraced the professional development plan and the required changes to the status quo. However, over time the level of professional conversations within the department meetings resulted in some attitudinal shifts that were identified through staff, student, and parent surveys used in the evaluation process. Some of those teachers with time constraints due to athletics and other extracurricular supervision responsibilities took advantage of the online professional development opportunities. A number of teachers enrolled in content-specific university courses to upgrade their subject matter knowledge. Ongoing classroom observations, portfolios, logs, surveys, and conversations with site administrators indicated the gradual assimilation of specific strategies into the repertoire of each teacher to address the learning needs of English Learners, students with disabilities, and those with special learning needs (GATE, below grade-level readers, etc.).

Points to Consider

In developing and implementing a professional development plan, consider the following:

- Develop a systematic professional development plan as part of the overall Single School Plan and clearly communicate the plan to all stakeholders.
- Develop the professional development plan around the identified skills and knowledge needed to accomplish the goals and objectives outlined in the Single School Plan, and always with the ultimate goal of improving student achievement.
- Ensure that professional development decisions are based on a review of current research of proven best practices, particularly at the secondary school level.
- Just as students have different experiences, needs, and existing skills and knowledge, the instructional staff also represents a wide range of skills, knowledge, and experience. The professional development plan should include a differentiated array of ways for teachers to identify and address their own learning needs.
- Consider including a variety of professional development opportunities beyond the traditional workshop approach. These might include development of portfolios, participation in district support programs for beginning teachers, university classes, online classes, and action research.
- Be sure that your professional development plan incorporates a systematic evaluation component that includes a needs assessment, multiple data sources (e.g., staff and student surveys,

observational data, portfolios, logs, workshop evaluations, etc.), timelines for data review, and mechanisms to adjust the plan, as needed.

- Review and access all available resources to support the implementation of your professional development plan. Remember to keep in mind human resources and time considerations. Providing a structured set of essential questions to guide department-meeting conversations will result in a professional development experience focused on improving student achievement.

- Access resources and support from the County Office of Education and universities in the area, as well as online professional development opportunities.

- Review the school's professional development plan with district office staff that administer and manage the state and federal budgets. They may have access to additional funds to support your efforts.

- There may be some parts of the school's professional development plan that will require negotiation or consultation with the bargaining unit. Review the plan with the Human Resources staff to identify and address those areas.

- Develop and communicate a defined application process for staff members to request professional development activities such as conference attendance, online workshops, or university classes.

- Include a professional development component as part of each teacher's annual goals.

- Identify, recruit, and systematically develop teacher leaders at your site.

- Invest in a full-day substitute to cover various peer observations by teachers throughout the day. For frequent use of a full-day sub, consider hiring a permanent sub for designated days (such as Tuesday, Wednesday, and Thursday).

- Instead of using an entire six-hour block of time on a Saturday, consider using three two-hour (or two three-hour) chunks of time after school, in the evening, or on Saturday mornings to offer ongoing professional development opportunities. This provides time for teachers to obtain and practice new information in "chunks," come back to discuss what worked and what didn't, and share information with each other. If your state or district provides professional development days, compensated or not, this model allows the school to maximize its professional development time by mixing and matching to meet its needs.

- Whenever possible, include peer coaching (observations, collaborative review of student data, and reflective conversations) as part of the professional development plan. If you can't afford a full-time coach, build in some release time during the day for teachers to observe each other and for coaching to occur.
- Don't forget that peer coaching is a skill. It is essential to provide specific and ongoing training to coaches on facilitating coaching conversations, pedagogy, how to collect observational data, data analysis, and so on. Ignoring this component will result in ineffective (at the least) or damaging (at the worst) coaching support.
- Effective principals and co-administrators attend and actively participate in professional development opportunities, whether they are workshops, department meetings, or ad hoc meetings to improve classroom practice. Teachers notice if you're not there and conclude that you don't think it's important.
- Consider having a point person at the site in charge of the myriad details inherent in organizing and implementing professional development opportunities at the site. A professional development checklist will greatly facilitate this process.

 ## Case Study 2: Connecting Teacher Needs to Professional Development

Greenview Middle School

In developing her Single School Plan during the summer, Mary included a professional development plan because it was a required part of the school plan. Because she already knew what workshops she would be providing to the staff on the three designated staff development days, it was relatively easy to tag those workshops onto the school plan. Specifically, she had contracted with two nationally recognized speakers to provide one-day workshops on multicultural sensitivity and differentiated instruction, respectively. Mary had heard both speakers at state conferences and thought they were excellent.

The first professional development day occurred prior to the beginning of school, when the school plan was presented and explained, and departments were provided with time to meet for some initial planning. National presenters provided the next two days of training, scheduled on a Saturday at the end of the first and second quarter. Mary was unable to attend these workshops due to prior commitments. Unfortunately, the national presenters were quite expensive and drained most of her professional development funds. In addition to these workshops, Mary provided each teacher with a list of district-sponsored workshops outlined in the *Staff Development Catalog.*

Mary expected her department chairs to follow up with teachers during department meetings. However, the department chairs were unclear about what they should actually do to follow up during the department meetings. Conversations in these meetings typically focused on day-to-day issues such as textbook distribution, testing schedules, and problems teachers were having with special education and English Learner students not learning the subject matter content. Few solutions were offered for these issues; the general consensus being that these students shouldn't be in the classes to start with if they didn't have the prerequisite academic and process skills.

Mary required a professional development plan as part of each teacher's annual goals. The plan was to reflect the site and district workshops outlined in the *Staff Development Catalog.* Although the district also offered mentor teacher support to beginning teachers and teachers new to the district, most of the mentors were teachers from other schools due to Mary's failure to adequately recruit mentors from her own staff and, in fact, failure to advertise the openings and application deadline in the staff bulletins. Mary was unclear about the goals and desired outcomes of the mentoring program, and she frequently cancelled scheduled observations (for on-site mentors) and follow-up reflective meetings due to lack of substitute teachers.

When Mary reviewed the workshop evaluations and a staff survey at the end of the first semester, the data indicated that although some teachers participated in the site workshops (they were offered on designated staff development Saturdays), they didn't perceive them as beneficial to their own work. Workshop participation could best be characterized as nonparticipatory, with teachers reading the paper, engaging in side conversations off topic, and frequently taking restroom and refreshment breaks. Data from the district office indicated that fewer than 10 percent of staff members participated in district-offered workshops. Mary's own classroom observations indicated that little or none of the information was being incorporated into classroom practice. Beginning teachers and mentors alike complained of the frequent classroom observation cancellations, resulting in an eventual absence of follow-through on program activities. Overall, the schools' professional development program was viewed by staff as fragmented, irrelevant, and a waste of time.

Points to Consider

- Beware of having (1) no professional development plan, or (2) a professional development plan that does not address the specific goals and objectives of the Single School Plan. The goals of the school plan provide the lens through which the staff can assess their individual needs.

- Beware of developing and implementing a professional development plan in isolation. Although this may expedite the process, you as the administrator represent only one viewpoint and one set of experiences. Even though it takes longer to work with a group of stakeholder representatives, the conversation will be richer and will more directly address the needs and concerns of the staff.

- Be sure that all staff members have the opportunity to provide specific input into the type of staff development that would be most valuable to them, as well as input regarding the logistical considerations such as date and time, location, duration, and so forth.

- Move beyond the one-shot workshop approach. Examine ways for teachers to collaboratively follow through into actual implementation of new strategies and academic content.

- The professional development plan should include a systematic process for evaluating the effectiveness of the overall program. This information should be shared with the staff and parent representatives. The most common mistakes made by site administrators are not having a clear program evaluation process and not sharing the information with stakeholders as part of systematically monitoring, assessing, and revising reform efforts.

- One size does not fit all. Provide a range of opportunities to engage teachers with varying experiences, interests, and time commitments.

- A common mistake made by site administrators is to delegate the planning and implementation of professional development activities solely to teacher leaders. Principal leadership is essential.

- Your presence as an active learner in professional development activities is critical to the importance staff will place on these activities.

- Professional development is most effective when it is job-embedded and available on-site.

Summary

A systematic, comprehensive professional development program is essential to successfully changing the culture of a school. The professional development program should be specifically designed to improve the achievement of all students and to provide the tools and strategies to make that happen. Effective professional development expands beyond the traditional one-shot "sit 'n' git" workshop to include ongoing, job-embedded opportunities for staff to engage in professional conversations around classroom instruction, assessment, and student learning. Effective secondary school principals provide the leadership to engage all stakeholders in the planning, development, monitoring, and evaluation of professional development based on stated school goals and objectives. The ultimate goal is improving student academic achievement.

Application Activity

1. What is the vision of the school, and how is it represented in the goals of the Single School Plan?

2. How does the professional development program at your school align with school goals and objectives?

3. What data are you using to assess professional development needs, and what *are* the professional development needs?

4. What time is already allotted for professional development? How can you create additional time to provide ongoing learning conversations among staff?

5. What evaluation system is in place to monitor the professional development program?

6. What might you want to add to the current system?

5

Professional Learning Communities

Using a Brain-Based Approach

It seems logical to the public that schools would become professional learning communities. Aren't educators in the business of teaching and learning? Aren't schools accountable for meeting professional standards? Yet, many secondary schools represent a collection of individuals and traditions without a sense of identity, connection, trust, or rapport.

In the previous chapters, we have asked the reader to become conscious of the impact of hidden attributes such as culture and the change process before embarking on the task of identifying school needs and developing a plan to implement school reform. Individuals participating in the reform initiative interpret these hidden attributes through the lens of their personal attitudes, values, and beliefs. Effective school leaders provide the structure for the school staff to recognize the hidden attributes and design a common vision to use to identify school needs and implement school reform.

Chapters 3 and 4 provide school leaders with some concrete strategies to consider when putting together a professional development plan and Single School Plan. These chapters identify people and networks to put in place to ensure stakeholders are given opportunities to participate in the reform process.

There are a number of resources available for school leaders to learn more about professional learning communities. During the past decade, many authors and speakers at national, state, and local educational conferences have spoken about the need for schools to become professional learning organizations or communities, built around a common interest using functional structures, systems, and procedures for implementing school reform. Many of the books and speeches highlight strategies that come from business and industry. Some of those strategies, such as site-based management and school leadership teams, have worked for educational leaders.

Leading effective secondary school reform requires a stable leadership in order to create an environment conducive to change. Schools are complex and interconnected networks that require adaptive systems. They must have leaders to guide, monitor, and assess the reform process at all times.

This chapter will build on the existing model of a professional learning community using research about the brain and examining how learning and thinking complement the research about developing professional learning communities. The following analogy is presented for school leaders to use with individuals having a difficult time visualizing the purpose and the complexity of a professional learning community.

Analogy: The School as an Individual

If we imagine the school as an individual, then the school's vision is the skeleton that defines what that "individual" will look like. The mission statement defines the identity and the purpose of the individual. Culture influences the beliefs and attitudes of the individual and ultimately the choices made during the growth of the organization. The action plan adds flesh to the skeletal structure, and professional development provides the nutrients for the individual to grow and flourish.

The Professional Learning Community as the Brain

Continuing this analogy, the professional learning community represents the brain. The professional learning community, like the brain, is a complex, interconnected, adaptive system. The majority of what we know about the brain and how it works has been learned over the past 25 years. President George H. W. Bush declared the 1990s as the decade of the brain, and a wealth of research occurred. "Applying this knowledge improves an individual's ability to access, retain, and use information, thereby expanding the opportunities to become more efficient and productive in our daily lives" (Alexander, 2003).

Coming on the heels of Paul MacLean's 1950s finding that most human behavior is the result of cooperation between the three systems of the brain—the R-complex or reptilian, the limbic, and the neocortex—known as the Triune Brain Theory (see www.kheper.net/topics/intelligence/MacLean.htm#triune), brain research in the 1960s and 1970s by Roger Sperry and Robert Ornstein led to the discovery that the two sides of the brain (right and left cortices) are linked by a complex network of fibers and control different types of mental activity (Buzan, 1991). This hemispheric research led to the work on left- and right-brained learning traits later used in many teacher preparation courses.

During the late 1970s, Ned Herrmann's research supported the findings that the functions of the brain are overlapping and interconnected. Herrmann designed the Herrmann Brain Dominance Instrument that measures the preferred ways and modes of thinking. This research expanded the hemispheric research by describing the four modes of thinking as the following: the upper mode (more cognitive and intellectual, preferring thinking in abstract, conceptual terms), the right mode (more intuitive and perceptive thinking, as well as idealistic, expressive, open approaches), the lower mode (more grounded, emotional, and instinctual in nature), and the left mode (preferring concise, efficient processes with realistic, disciplined, and orderly approaches) (The Ned Herrmann Group, 1985).

The brain, like a professional learning community, processes information and makes situational decisions relying on facts, intuition, emotions, and tradition. If information is weighted in favor of any one of the four variables listed above, then the decision and outcome will be different. A professional learning community recognizes and appreciates the uniqueness and interconnectedness of these variables and finds time to develop the skills and appreciate the wisdom of each approach and the impact it has on improving student achievement.

Furthermore, school leaders are being held accountable to the standards of both an organization and a community. An "organization" is often measured by its efficiency, expediency, and increased productivity; whereas the standards of a "community" place greater emphasis on relationships, shared ideas, and a strong culture (DuFour & Eaker, 1998). The challenge is not in "what is measured," but in what the agencies and people in power *value* as valid and reliable processes and data. Experience suggests that "organizations" tend to value facts and traditions, while "communities" tend to value intuition and emotions. *Facts and traditions* are more likely to be traits of left-brained thinkers; *intuition and emotions* tend to be traits of right-brained thinkers.

In order to meet accountability standards, it is important for school leaders to understand what is valued and rewarded by the public and elected officials. If a school leader focuses on "community" when the public values student performance data, then "success" will be difficult. By using brain research, it is possible to develop systems so that the organization can meet the standards of both and communicate the accomplishments using the language that is valued and rewarded by all stakeholders.

What *Is* a Professional Learning Community?

The foundation of a professional learning community is built upon the vision, mission, values, and goals of a school (DuFour & Eaker, 1998). Peter Senge et al. (2000) further explain that professional learning communities are characterized by a clear sense of direction and purpose, where every effort is made to reduce the sense of isolation by connecting people and information and providing powerful methods and tools for staff to develop new skills and capabilities.

The following description of *professional, learning,* and *community* forms the basis of our definition.

- **Professional**—meeting the standards of a profession. Words used to describe "professional" include qualified, licensed, skilled, and trained.
- **Learning**—coming to know or know how. Words used to describe "learning" include knowledge, education, sophisticated, and complex.
- **Community**—a group with common interests. Words used to describe "community" include identity, connection, and rapport.

Therefore, one definition might be that a professional learning community is a group of people with a shared interest in the knowledge, application, and improvement of professional education standards.

Roots of the Professional Learning Community

The roots of the professional learning community can be found in Edwards Deming's Total Quality Management and Continuous

Process Improvement work from the 1940s and 1950s. In his work, Demming stresses the importance of setting up teams to analyze problems and identify strategies to improve the quality of an organization's product. He also emphasizes that quality is the responsibility of everyone in the organization, and therefore success is dependent on having a well-trained and motivated staff focused on continuous improvement.

Among the books written about developing learning communities, Richard DuFour and Robert Eaker's book, *Professional Learning Communities at Work* (1998), describes how to reorganize schools into learning communities. In the book, DuFour and Eaker identify six characteristics of the professional learning community.

1. *Shared mission, vision, and values.* A shared commitment and understanding about the direction, purpose, and standards for the school.

2. *Collective inquiry.* A belief that the status quo is not good enough. Individuals in a learning community value the questioning, searching, discovering, experimenting, and reflecting cycle of learning and improving.

3. *Collaborative teams.* Groups of people with common interests in increasing their capacity for learning. Collaborative teams learn from each other, apply the knowledge, and then reflect on the process in order to improve the status quo.

4. *Action orientation and experimentation.* One of the key characteristics that separate learning communities from underperforming schools is the belief that improvement occurs when people are willing to experiment and take action to change the attitudes and beliefs that have contributed to the decline of student achievement. Inaction is not an option.

5. *Continuous improvement.* Members of a learning community constantly search for ideas, strategies, and systems to improve the way teachers teach and students learn.

6. *Results orientation.* The results of the professional learning team are measurable, are tangible, and provide the basis for the next phase of school improvement.

A professional learning community embraces and uses a cycle of learning and improving. Teacher preparation programs use a variation of this cycle of learning as the basis of the "Plan, Teach,

Reflect, Apply" model (California Department of Education, 2003) for designing learning experiences for students. Corporate organizations also use a variation of this cycle through the Total Quality Management process.

If we combine our knowledge and understanding of the research behind quality management, continuous improvement, and how the brain works, then the analogy of the brain as a professional learning community makes sense. Interconnectedness and adaptability are strengths of both the brain and a professional learning community.

Steps to Consider When Establishing a Professional Learning Community

- Identify the hidden attributes of the culture of your school
- Review the change process with the entire staff
- Review the vision and mission statement with the entire staff
- Identify expected outcomes for students
- Identify common goals for the staff to focus on for the year
- Identify how your school will know when it has reached a goal
- Identify how your school will celebrate success

Case Studies

The following case studies illustrate two different approaches to building a professional learning community. In one case, the principal has had time to identify the professional development needed to move the staff to the next stage in the evolution of building community. In the second case, the principal uses existing structures on campus to promote collegiality but miscommunicates the efforts to the superintendent.

 **Case Study 1: Identifying the Right Professional Development**

Ridge View Middle School
　　Principal Tony R. has just completed his second year at Ridge View Middle School. His faculty advisory team, composed of the two

co-administrators and representatives from each of the departments, established a professional development calendar at the end of the previous year. The professional development plan identified one preservice day to work on the action research project (Chapter 7, Action Research) and two preservice days to explore the concepts of a professional learning community.

Last year, while conducting research for the Single School Plan, the faculty advisory team met with teachers from a different school who believed that the professional development that combined brain research and organizational development assisted the faculty's evolution into a professional learning community. The team chose to use some of Ridge View Middle School's categorical funds to hire an external consultant to facilitate a two-day workshop to learn more about a brain-based approach to developing a professional learning community. Several members of the faculty advisory team hoped the new approach would spark the curiosity of the veteran faculty who had become cynical about efforts to improve student performance. The faculty advisory team advertised this professional development workshop as, "Improving student performance and teacher satisfaction with less effort."

The first day of professional development was devoted to understanding more about the brain's ability to grow and learn, how the likelihood for success can be increased, how the brain operates, and how to exercise the brain for greater productivity. The second day of the workshop explored how to expand the concepts learned in the first day from an individual perspective to an organizational perspective. Student performance data and accountability measures were provided to "teams" with the intention of generating solutions to improve student achievement for groups of students identified to be in greatest need. Teams took time to get to know each other's style preferences for thinking in different situations before they tackled the data and generated solutions. At the end of the second day, each team proposed several learning strategies identified in the brain research to improve student achievement for the two student subgroups in greatest need, special education students and English language learners. The faculty prioritized the suggestions and included the first two in the Single School Plan.

At the end of each quarter, Tony met with the faculty advisory team and shared the results of the student benchmark performance data collected. The team was encouraged with the increase in the improvement of the special education students after using the whole-brain reading strategies. English language learners performed at a higher level than the previous year; however, the committee suggested that the "teams" come back together and create additional learning strategies to use in the second semester.

Additional recommendations by the team included scheduling ongoing grade-level and departmental conversations between teachers of core subjects and electives to review student assessment data and discuss progress of special education students and English learners. Time would also be scheduled for teachers to review lesson plans and examine student work using a specific inquiry protocol to maintain focus. Minutes of these meetings would be submitted to Tony to keep him apprised of progress.

Tony realized that the action research project and school improvement teams had provided greater opportunities for the teachers to work and learn together. The shared vision for student improvement had led to a greater ownership in the education of students at Ridge View Middle School. For the first time in a year, Tony was hopeful that progress was being made to focus on student learning.

Points to Consider

- Professional learning communities experience greater success when staff is provided with professional development to acquire the knowledge, skills, and motivation to effectively solve problems.
- Remember, learners are not experts. Learning is a process during which mistakes will occur. Provide support for risk taking.
- Find time in the school calendar for staff to learn together. Suggestions for "finding time" are included in Chapter 4, Professional Development.
- Professional learning communities are more likely to be effective if they focus on a clear goal for improving the achievement of all students.
- Moving from a culture of isolation to that of a learning community is a massive paradigm shift in secondary schools. It takes time and support for those engaged in the process.
- Encourage the development of departmental learning teams that regularly review their subject's benchmark and teacher-generated student assessment data with the goal of improving instruction.
- Articulate goals in terms of measurable outcomes.

- Identify and articulate the values and beliefs about improving the achievement of all students that define your school as a community.
- Translate those values into professional standards.
- Hold staff accountable for meeting professional standards and obligations.

 ## Case Study 2: Communicating Professional Development Efforts

Birch Knoll High School

Principal Carl A. believes in the importance of teamwork. He believes that a successful leader can motivate a group by articulating the goals to improve student achievement and providing the structure for accomplishing those goals. Over the past three years, Carl has been a co-administrator at Birch Knoll High School and is familiar with the disconnection between the faculty and administration. This is Carl's first year as a principal and he wants to communicate the efforts of the committees on campus in order to promote a big picture of what is occurring at the school.

In a letter to the superintendent, Carl outlined the efforts currently underway at Birch Knoll High School toward developing a professional learning community. Carl pointed out that his intention was to work with the existing committees and coach them toward a shared goal of improving student achievement. Carl cited the progress of the following committees:

- The Action Plan Committee completed the school plan for the current year and is excited about its efforts.
- The School Safety Committee completed an analysis of last year's incident reports and submitted recommendations for changes to the student behavior code to the School Site Council.
- The School-Community Partnership Committee scheduled a meeting in March to discuss this year's school beautification project.
- The Faculty Advisory Committee has been given time at the next staff meeting to discuss the upcoming visit of the state improvement team.

- The math department has agreed to participate in an action research project to determine if student achievement is greater when teachers align the curriculum to the standardized assessment test.
- The student government has recommended that the school hold an educational summit prior to spring break to discuss the new graduation requirements.

Carl further explained that he intended to be present at each of the upcoming meetings to share the vision of the school and discuss the role of each person as a part of that vision. Carl invited the superintendent to visit the school to see firsthand the efforts of the staff and students.

Carl provided each staff member with a copy of the letter. Several staff members stopped by his office to thank him for recognizing the work being accomplished by faculty. Carl also heard staff members planning time to meet to discuss agenda topics for upcoming meetings.

Three weeks after Carl sent the letter to the district, he received a note from the superintendent. In the note, the superintendent pointed out that although the work of existing committees was a good idea, he wanted to know how the committees were developing into professional learning communities. Furthermore, the superintendent requested a list of the assessments Carl was using to gather data to demonstrate improved student achievement.

Carl was stunned that the superintendent didn't see how the efforts of the committees were leading to the development of a professional learning community. He went home that night worrying about how to continue to improve the morale of the staff while shifting his focus to gathering student performance data.

Points to Consider

- Take time to identify what is valued and rewarded by the superintendent and the board of education to ensure school and district priorities are aligned.
- Identify exactly what accountability measures you will need to address in your Single School Plan, such as academic improvement targets in language arts and mathematics by student subgroups.
- Identify common goals for the staff to focus on throughout the year.

- Identify the purpose for each school committee. Is there any duplication of effort?
- In the example above, Carl clearly was making progress toward improving the morale of the staff; however, he might have received more support from the superintendent if he had outlined the committee work as tasks of the action plan goals. In addition, if Carl had used more procedural and numeric phrases rather than emotional terms, his information might have better aligned with the values of the district.

Summary

In this chapter, we explored the analogy that compared a professional learning community to the brain. We acknowledged that a brain is a complex, interconnected, adaptive system. A professional learning community is also a complex, interconnected, adaptive system that values a strong vision, efficiency, and increased productivity as well as acknowledging the importance of culture and relationships.

A professional learning community is a group of people with a shared interest in the knowledge, application, and improvement of professional education standards with a clear goal of improving student achievement. Professional growth is a norm of professional learning communities. There is a clear sense of direction, purpose, and connection between people and information. Inaction is no longer an option for effective schools. A professional learning community believes in the importance of action and experimentation in order to grow and learn. Professional learning communities expect the best and learn from the rest.

Application Activity

1. What structures are currently in place at your school to support a professional learning community? (Site-based management teams, school leadership teams, etc.)

2. How can you incorporate some dedicated time in your master schedule and school calendar for teachers to meet and engage in professional conversations?

3. What protocols, or group norms, are in place for structured learning conversations?

4. How do you and your staff organize time to collaboratively assess student work on an ongoing basis? How does this work inform instruction?

5. What professional development is needed to ensure staff has the skills and knowledge to engage in meaningful conversations about teaching and learning, as well as enhance instruction to meet student needs?

6. How will you know if these learning conversations are taking place and if they are making a difference?

6

Parent
Involvement

The Missing Link

Remember when you sent your child to school for the first time? You probably attended PTA meetings, parent conferences, and every assembly, play, or carnival that came along. Historically, parent involvement remains strong through the primary and intermediate grades and tends to slow down by about the 6th grade. By the time kids reach the middle school level, it's much more difficult to get parents to participate in school-related activities.

The term "parent involvement" refers to the willingness of the parent to demonstrate commitment to and participation in the education of his or her child in relation to the school (LaBahn, 1995). Using this definition, examples of parent involvement might include attending a scheduled meeting such as an IEP, student registration, or discipline conference with a teacher or administrator; attending a school event such as Back to School Night, athletic events, or musical presentations; or serving the school through volunteer work or participation on a school committee.

Regardless of the difficulty in obtaining strong parent involvement at the secondary level, there is a growing recognition that the school-parent partnership is an essential component of a child's education. There is evidence that family involvement, not just socioeconomic status, is critical to student success (Henderson & Berla, 1994). Federal legislation such as *No Child Left Behind Act* of 2001 *requires* that schools provide opportunities for parents to be involved in the decision making and support of their child's education.

This chapter outlines a variety of ideas, suggestions, and resources that will support secondary administrators in providing a parent- and family-friendly environment, ways to expand and improve communication to the home and community, and ways for parents to get involved or volunteer at the school.

Why Aren't Parents Involved?

As stated in the opening paragraphs of this chapter, parents of elementary school-age children tend to be much more involved with the children's education and the school. This involvement noticeably slackens as students reach middle school and high school. Typically, parents start attending fewer important decision-making conferences such as IEP meetings, enrollment meetings, post-secondary planning meetings with school counselors, and discipline meetings. Why does this happen?

Adolescent Autonomy

Remember the days when the elementary teachers pinned notices of parent conferences, PTA meetings, and school carnivals to your coat and told you to give them to your mother? Every parent of a teenager can tell you that the older the child gets, the more he or she excludes parents from pertinent information about what's happening in his or her life. As a natural part of growing up, secondary students begin to demand autonomy and often attempt to restrict the information flow from school to home. This is particularly true if there is a problem, such as a classroom discipline issue, poor academic performance on a test, failure to turn in homework on a regular basis, or frequent absences. In their quest for autonomy, many students routinely scan the mail each day before their parents get home and confiscate anything that comes from the school. There is no question that secondary schools must develop strong two-way communication links with parents to ensure they are involved in monitoring and supporting the academic achievement of their children.

Negative School-Related Experiences During Their Own Education

Many parents are not eager to interact with secondary schools because of their own negative experiences during middle school and/or high school. There are many parents, particularly in Title I schools in low socioeconomic neighborhoods, who either dropped out of high school or graduated without the necessary academic skills and knowledge to successfully navigate higher education or the adult world. These negative experiences can and will carry over into attitudes and beliefs about school and its impact on their own children. These are often reinforced by school communications that provide only negative information, such as discipline referrals or class failure notices, about their children. Understandably, parents with negative experiences tend to either withdraw from or limit contact with schools and school personnel, or they interact with suspicion and anger. Involving them in school activities, events, or proceedings requires one-on-one, positive personal communication by teachers and administrators. Parents need to perceive that (1) school is a safe place for them and their child (from real or perceived staff and/or student bullies); (2) they (the parents) are welcome at the school; (3) their participation is necessary in promoting the success of their children; and that (4) school personnel care about their children and wish to work with parents in partnership to promote student success. This chapter will discuss some specific strategies that may be incorporated at secondary schools to make this happen.

Skewed Priorities

Many parents today simply don't place a high priority on school attendance if other activities interfere. While many students miss school on a regular basis for scheduled doctor or dentist appointments, greater numbers than ever before are coming in late, leaving early, or missing days at a time due to sleeping in, shopping for a prom dress, celebrating non-calendared holidays, or taking a family skiing vacation in January.

Lack of Information on How to Get Involved

There are parents who genuinely want to become more involved at the school, but simply don't know how. If they haven't been involved in parent activities at their child's elementary or middle school, they don't have the network for that kind of involvement at the next level. Communication links are essential to increasing parent participation.

The Sheer Size of Secondary Schools

Elementary schools, for the most part, are much smaller, warmer, and more nurturing than secondary schools. The transition to middle school is often difficult due to the larger population of the school, resulting in a disruption of the established personal relationships and "pecking order" for both students and parents. Add to that the move from a single teacher to five to seven different teachers throughout the day. Two years later, students again transition into schools that often range from 2,000 to 4,000+ students. What is overwhelming for the students can also be overwhelming for the parents, who often have difficulty knowing the location of campus offices and classrooms or whom to contact when they have questions or concerns. Effective school leaders—both teachers and administrators—actively address the issue of individualizing student and parent support and find ways to systematically engage parents in the child's educational experience.

Creating a Family-Friendly Secondary School

Family-friendly schools have specific policies that delineate the importance of parent involvement, as well as a wide range of ways parents might be involved that don't require extensive amounts of time or commitment. As the site principal or instructional leader, there are some specific steps you can take to open up the school to parents; establish two-way communication; and identify opportunities for training, volunteerism, and involvement in decision making.

Welcoming Environment

As stated earlier in this chapter, many parents are intimidated by the sheer size of a secondary school campus. This is often exacerbated by the fact that most secondary school students don't want their parents to set foot on the campus. Not only are campuses often confusing labyrinths of buildings, corridors, fields, and quads, but they also are often unattractive, dirty, and "institutional." As a school leader, it's important to create a welcoming, inclusive environment for parents and make them feel comfortable being at the school.

- Post signs welcoming parents and community members to the campus. Use language on the signs that is inviting rather than directive regarding checking in at the front office. Include signs in Spanish or other primary language, if appropriate.
- Take overt steps to reach out to parents. Some schools have a Community Attendance Worker who makes appointments to visit parents in the home throughout the year.
- Have visitor badges available for outside visitors to the campus.
- Set aside a room or a section of the library as a Parent Resource Center, with access to a copy machine, and magazines, books, and other resource materials that are available to parents for checkout.
- Be sensitive to parent working hours by keeping some scheduled weekend or evening office hours.
- Offer a Parent Institute on parenting skills and strategies. If appropriate, be sure to include a Spanish or other primary language version. At the least, have translators and special needs support available. Ensure you have childcare available.
- Provide "Family Nights," with themed events that provide opportunities for students to perform, exhibit their work, or participate in a support capacity. Examples might include cultural awareness events, an academic fair, a Renaissance Fair, or a Family Literacy Night, with breakout sessions for parents, as well as younger brothers and sisters. Students facilitate the breakouts, along with teachers and administrators.
- Recognize and thank parents for the work that they do with their students. This might be done through letters home, phone calls, and parent volunteer recognition activities.

Communication

Clear, effective communication with parents and community is an ongoing issue at secondary schools. It is frequently cited as an area for improvement by accreditation and program-review visiting committees. Parents often perceive communications as one-way, with little opportunity for two-way conversations to take place.

Establish an expectation that switchboard operators, attendance clerks, secretaries, administrators, and teachers maintain a welcoming, positive, pleasant, and helpful tone in telephone, e-mail, and face-to-face communications with parents and community. If parents are already intimidated about contacting the school, a rude employee can further exacerbate the impression that the school is not a welcoming place for parents.

Welcome/Orientation meetings for parents of new students: This is especially critical in very large schools that have many students enrolling throughout the year. Hold an evening meeting each month (or quarter) for parents of new students, with coffee, refreshments, and childcare services available. The meeting should include a tour of the school; a quick review of key information such as the school calendar, discipline system, and academic requirements; and a testing schedule with accompanying handouts for later reference. Students make great tour guides and can answer questions about the school from a student's perspective.

Handbooks/Newsletters: Even though most secondary schools have both, they are not always effectively utilized. In addition to information about the calendar, policies, and programs, include specific information on ways that parents can support their student's academic success. Also include information on opportunities for parents to become actively involved in the school.

Ensure that all newsletters, handbooks, and legal forms (such as IEP forms) are available in other languages, if appropriate. There are greater numbers of Spanish-speaking parents than ever before with children in the public education system. Having important information in the primary language allows parents to better connect with the school and the educational experiences of their children.

School Web site: Most schools now have Web sites, but they are often underutilized. Some ways you can increase communication through your school's Web site include the following:

- A message from the principal gives you, the principal, an opportunity to set the stage for the overall mission of the school.
- School vision and mission statements, as well as the school plan, provide vital information on the priorities of the school.
- Include the school's accountability report card, with data about student performance, teacher credentialing, and so forth. Each state has different requirements in this area.
- Provide updated information on benchmark testing results in the core areas to keep parents apprised of progress.
- Include the school handbook, information brochures, calendar, lunch menu, activities calendar, scholarship information, and the testing calendar.
- Let parents and family "Meet the staff" through bios, class schedules, contact information, e-mail links, and even virtual introductions by

staff members themselves, along with video clips of actual classroom instruction. Many teachers have already set up their own Web sites, with homework links and e-mail links.

- Include a Volunteer Opportunities section, with descriptions of the various opportunities available at the school, the time commitment required, and contact information (phone and e-mail).
- Include information about student clubs and organizations, the club advisors, eligibility criteria, and contact information.
- Include an Alumni Corner, with information, events, and news about alumni.
- Include a Parent Tips section, with suggestions about how parents can support their students. Include links to various parent Web sites such as the PTA.
- Highlight specific programs; academies; student organizations; and student, teacher, or classified Employee of the Month, with pictures, bios, and sample projects.
- Highlight specific departments, with homework support links.

Adapted from Jeffrey Richter's *Principal's Guide to Effective Family Involvement: Partnering for School Success*, Aspen Publishers, 2002, p. 1.

Schedule short "Coffees" in the evenings throughout the year (3 to 4 times), held at the homes of parent volunteers who provide coffee and light refreshments. Lasting about an hour, these coffees provide an opportunity for parents to meet the school leader(s) and engage in a more informal dialogue about the school. When meeting with parents who are not English speakers, ensure that a translator is available.

Volunteer to speak to community service organizations such as Rotary and Kiwanis, Human Relations Task Force, church organizations that represent your community, American Association of University Women, and racial/ethnic organizations such as the Hispanic Chamber of Commerce and the NAACP. These organizations have program chairs that are always looking for interesting and relevant speakers. Every one of those organizations has members with children in your school, or graduates whom they employ.

Parents as Learning Partners

For the most part, parents want their students to be academically successful and graduate from high school. The accountability requirements of the *No Child Left Behind Act* of 2001, as well as individual state requirements, have resulted in a real concern by some parents that their children may not qualify for a high school diploma. Academic content standards have become quite rigorous, with many parents feeling they are unable to support their children in helping them with homework. This is particularly true when students move into higher-level math and science. Some strategies for supporting student learning include the following:

- Ensure that parents (as well as students) are thoroughly informed of the academic content standards for each of their child's courses. This can be accomplished during Back to School Night classroom visits, at parent-orientation meetings, in standards pamphlets for each course, through highlights in the Principal's Newsletter, as a link on the school's Web site, during parent advisory meetings, and at booster club meetings (when discussing eligibility). Be sure the standards are available in Spanish, or other primary language, as appropriate.

- Provide evening or Saturday morning tutoring workshops for parents in specific areas of the curriculum, so that they, in turn, can tutor their children. For example, most states now have an algebra requirement for all secondary students. Many parents have forgotten, or never mastered, algebra. By taking 2- to 3-hour workshops twice a month, parents can renew the necessary skills and knowledge in the content area based on the topics being taught to their children at that time, and learn strategies on how to assist them.

Involving Parents/Community in the Decision-Making Process

As stated earlier, a requirement of most federal and state programs is the inclusion of parents in the decision-making process. Parents are critical stakeholders at the school, and their input is valuable in the areas of school planning, curricular and career program advisement, instructional materials selection, school safety, and student activities. *Parents involved in any decision-making activities must clearly understand the time commitment and parameters of any committee or task force on which they serve.*

To encourage greater parent participation, distribute a Parent Interest Inventory during registration, at Back to School Night, in the Parent Handbook, and on the school's Web site to identify those parents who might be interested in participating as a member of school committees. Publish a meeting calendar for the year.

Case Studies

The following two case studies illustrate how a middle school principal and a high school principal address the challenge of getting parents involved in their children's education. The first case covers a wide range of activities designed to increase parent involvement at the high school level. The second case study explores the challenges of traditional parent-communication processes.

Case Study 1: Identifying Ways to Involve Parents

Municipal High School

   Municipal High School parent involvement has traditionally been through the School Site Council and on the Football and Band Booster Clubs. This year, however, Anna and the School Site Council have set a clear goal to increase parent involvement as a means to improve the participation by parents in the decision-making process. Three major goals were identified: considering parent input in the decision-making process, improving communication with all parents, and making the school more parent-friendly.

   Specific efforts were made to provide a welcoming environment for parents. Anna changed her principal letter in the Parent Handbook to specifically invite parents to become more involved in the school. She provided a workshop for clerical support staff—often the first people that parents interact with at a school site—to address expectations and strategies for positive communication with parents and community.

   Anna also developed a quarterly Newcomers' Reception for parents of new students, as well as a schedule of quarterly hour-long Principal Coffees, during which parents could drop by to discuss any issues related to the school. This also allowed Anna to talk to parents informally about the reform efforts that were occurring at the school. Anna highlighted the dates and issued an ongoing invitation in each of her monthly Principal Newsletters mailed to the home of every student. She also had the dates posted in the local newspaper's

Community Section and in the local Spanish-language newspaper. Childcare was made available at the Principal Coffees, provided by parent volunteers. Receptions and coffees have been well attended.

Anna has made a particular effort to include the parents of her Hispanic student population. A major project was undertaken with the District Office to provide key district/school documents and school signs in Spanish. Translators were made available for all parent workshops, meetings, and parent activities. Spanish-speaking volunteers made individual phone calls inviting parents to partici-pate on committees, parent workshops, and advisory teams. As a result, participation by Spanish-speaking parents has dramatically increased.

Familiar with the research findings that parents' support of their children's education resulted in improved academic success, Anna developed a Parent Institute and Parent Homework Tutorials on Saturday mornings to assist those parents who did not feel they had the necessary expertise in the content areas to help their children. These tutorials were available in Language Arts and Algebra I.

In an effort to improve school communication, Anna enlisted the help of the computer technology teacher and his Web Design class. They redesigned the school's Web site to include a variety of infor-mational topics, including the school calendar, a meeting calendar, parent workshops, and Parent Tips for Student Success. The Web site also highlighted the teacher, classified staff member, parent volunteer, and student of the month. The Web site is updated monthly, with input from the Parent Liaison and a PTA subcommittee.

Anna has initiated a concerted effort to increase communication with parents and the community. She recently spoke about the school and its reform initiatives to the Women's Club at the local church. That one appearance has resulted in a great deal of "chatter" among the parents and within the community about the reform efforts underway at Municipal High. She has scheduled two additional pre-sentations to community organizations over the course of the year. At the end of the first year, data indicated a significant increase in parent involvement in the school and school activities by all parents, espe-cially Hispanic parents.

Points to Consider

- Include parents with different viewpoints on advisory committees. Sometimes, the best way to soften particularly critical or agitated parents is to have them participate in the decision-making process. This only works if parents are willing to adhere to group decision-making norms.

- Recruit an interested parent to assist in the coordination of parent activities and programs.
- Your school's Web site is a very strong communication resource. Use it!

Case Study 2: Communicating With Parents

Greenview Middle School

As she was writing the school plan during the summer, Mary M. included a specific goal that addressed improving parent involvement and participation in the decision-making process. This was done to justify the expenditure of 10 percent of her Title I funds, as required, for parent involvement. Mary had appointed three parents to her School Site Council; all were parents of honors-level white students.

Mary considered Back to School Night moderately well attended, with 40 parents (enrollment at Greenview is 1200) attending. In addition, she mentioned special events and performances in her newsletter, resulting in sporadic attendance by parents. Some parents have complained that they work some distance away or have family commitments earlier in the evening and cannot attend school functions until 7:00 PM or after.

Quarterly newsletters are scheduled, but Mary frequently forgets to compose them until long past the quarterly date. She sent out two newsletters during the school year. Although she sent formal letters to Title I and Limited-English-Proficient parents, inviting them to participate on committees, only two or three people ever showed up for the meetings. Spanish-speaking parents in particular did not participate in school-related activities.

Mary and the faculty continue to identify lack of parent support as the primary reason for student underachievement. Parents, on the other hand, express frustration at the poor communication and the perceived lack of caring on the part of the school. Teachers frequently fail to return parent phone calls and often restrict communication with the home to the required quarterly progress reports.

Points to Consider

- In communicating with parents and community members, avoid using "educationeze" and jargon. In explaining educational information, use simple, easy-to-understand language.
- Remember to clearly communicate the time commitment for any parent involvement activities. More time will be required to serve on an advisory committee or School Site Council than for chaperoning one dance.
- Personal phone calls inviting parents to participate on advisory committees, chaperone dances, or serve on ad hoc committees are much more likely to result in parent participation. (Don't forget to use primary language callers if you are inviting Limited-English-Proficient parents.)
- Be sensitive to family commitments early in the evening. People are more willing to attend school events if they are held after the dinner hour.
- A major complaint from parents across the nation is that teachers do not return phone calls. Work with your staff to develop a norm of returning phone calls within 24 hours.

Summary

Federal and state legislation mandates that schools encourage and support participation by parents in their child's education. Research indicates that parent involvement results in improved student academic achievement. Although parent involvement significantly declines by the time students reach secondary school, there are some concrete steps that instructional leaders can take to change that dynamic. These steps include providing a welcoming, safe school environment; a two-way communication network; and a variety of opportunities for parents to become involved. It is essential that secondary principals and faculty implement a systematic parent-outreach program to bring parents into a partnership with the school to improve student achievement.

Application Activity

1. How welcoming would a parent find your school? What might you put into place to make your school more parent-friendly?

2. What training sessions do you have available for parents? What additional training might your school consider?

3. What mechanisms do you have in place to communicate with parents and community? What else might you do to improve communication?

4. What do you currently have in place to ensure that Limited-English-Speaking parents understand communications from the school?

5. How do you support faculty and staff in developing positive and effective parent-communication skills?

PART III

Assessment and Accountability

7

Action Research

Lights, Camera, Action Research!

Congratulations. Your planning team has developed a course of action for your school and staff. Your team has prepared a Single School Plan to accomplish the identified tasks. The site professional-development calendar has been created and you are ready to implement your Single School Plan.

But wait! Your superintendent has just asked you how you will know if the instructional strategies identified in your Single School Plan are working to improve student achievement. You quickly turn to your school plan and point out that one of the assessment measures your staff will make use of will be action research. Your superintendent is impressed, leaves your school confident you have a well-thought-out plan for the year, and looks forward to seeing your first interim report.

What *Is* Action Research?

Action research provides opportunities for stakeholders to examine incremental results of instructional interventions based on predetermined data points, analyze and reflect on the effectiveness of the teaching strategies, and determine instructional modifications as needed. For the purposes of this chapter, we will focus on instructional strategies for improving student performance.

Action research has been used in educational settings around the world for the purpose of school restructuring, professional growth, curriculum development, and collaboration between K–12 schools and universities. As early as 1946, Kurt Lewin introduced the idea of action research. Stephen Corey and others at the Teachers College of Columbia University introduced the term "action research" to the educational community in 1949. Corey (1953) defined action research as, "the process through which practitioners study their own practice to solve their personal practical problems."

Action research is usually conducted by a group of teachers. This "team" provides support and a forum for sharing questions, concerns, and results. Teachers advise each other and comment on the progress of individual efforts. "Engaging in collaborative action research helps eliminate the isolation that has long characterized teaching, as it promotes professional dialogue and thus, creates a more professional culture in schools" (Johnson, 1993).

Articles, essays, and books provide a wealth of background information, research, and case studies about Action Research, Collaborative Action Research, and Teacher as Researcher. In his book, *Guiding School Improvement With Action Research* (2000), Richard Sagor points out that teachers care most about their teaching and the development of their students. Action research provides opportunities for teachers to hold conversations about student learning based on student work and performance assessment data. Action research helps educators become more effective teachers.

Where Do I Start?

Here are six steps to consider when developing an action research project:

1. Assess the need.

   How will this project improve student performance (an indicator of student achievement)?

   What student performance data is valued and rewarded by the district? What assessment sources are currently used to gather this data?

2. Create an action plan (see Chapter 3).

   What task will this assessment project support?

   How will this project align with other projects mandated by the district and/or state?

3. Gather data from multiple sources.

   What staff and student work will be used to assess if students have learned the agreed-upon instructional objective?

4. Reflect on information.

   How does the data from student work samples align with current assessment data?

   What protocol will be used for action research conversations?

   What product will result from action research?

5. Revise/modify implementation as needed.

   Schedule staff meetings to review progress of the project, or include project progress reports as part of regular staff meetings.

6. Prepare a summative assessment report.

   What do the data and reflections tell us about student learning?

   How will the summative report findings be shared with all stakeholders?

How Can I Be Sure All Staff Understand the Action Research Process?

Prepare all staff with the knowledge and skills necessary to participate in the action research project through mini-workshops, department meetings, and professional literature. Some staff may be familiar with this concept if they have participated in a focus group for a coordinated compliance review or school accreditation. Enlist some of these staff members for your Action Research Project Team. It is a good idea to begin the discussion with the "big picture"—what is action research and how can it improve our teaching and students' learning? It is essential, however, to clearly define the structure, procedures, and products of the action research process and to communicate these components clearly to the staff.

Case Studies

The following case studies illustrate two very different approaches to incorporating action research taken by school principals. The first case study reveals a purposeful, well-thought-out plan to incorporate action research to inform instruction and improve student achievement. The second case study identifies how action research might be used to fulfill district mandates.

RVMS Case Study 1: Using Action Research to Inform Instruction

Ridge View Middle School

Principal Tony R. is looking forward to the beginning of the school year. His faculty and student representatives are prepared to engage in an action research project to study student work, in order to identify instructional strategies and best practices to increase student performance.

After careful research and planning, Tony's administrative team and the Faculty-Student Advisory Committee (FSAC) have created a plan to determine if using "teaching and learning check-in points" during the school year will improve performance on the annual state student performance assessment. The team decided to conduct an action research project and established the Action Research Project Team (ARPT) to lead the staff workshops. The team included department chairpersons as well as representatives from the guidance department, teachers' association, and student groups.

Last year, the Ridge View Middle School administrative team and the FSAC worked together to identify what data was valued and rewarded by the district, the community, and the state. Based on newspaper articles and district reports to the school board, the FSAC agreed that no matter how much a student was able to accomplish in the classroom, the bottom line for assessing the success of a school, in the eyes of the community, the district, and the state, was the results of the statewide student performance assessment.

The Action Research Project Team (ARPT) presented a report to the faculty at the beginning of the second semester, outlining the results of their research on public opinion and student performance data as an indicator for school success. Public opinion was gathered using a short survey to identify what students, staff, and parents believed were indicators of a successful school. The survey confirmed that test scores were important indicators of success. The ARPT examined the prior two years of disaggregated student-performance assessment data to identify learning trends. In addition, the team reviewed research about how other underperforming schools were tackling the issue of improving scores on high-stakes student performance assessments.

The team acknowledged in their findings to the faculty that report card grades were important to students, parents, and teachers. However, they noted that if the school's student performance assessment data, as reported on the school accountability report card, was not meeting the identified statewide expectations, then the community and elected officials were not satisfied with the results of the teaching and learning achievements. In other words, since student performance data was published in the newspapers each year, this data held more weight than grades on a report card. It was also noted that student grades in core classes were inconsistent with standardized test results, often reflecting higher grades than assessment results for the same student.

The team believed that reviewing student performance data trends could inform teaching and learning. The team recommended incorporating an action research project to examine student performance trends.

In its report, the team outlined a plan to use a preservice day plus 2 to 3 dedicated faculty work hours during the school year to accomplish the action research project. Following the report to the faculty, the project team reviewed a set of draft agendas for the Action Plan Work Sessions with the FSAC and then with the faculty at large. Each team member was responsible for keeping his or her department staff informed about the project at the monthly staff meetings. By June, the Ridge View Middle School staff had a clear picture of the action research project as well as its purpose, goals, and intended results.

Points to Consider

- Conduct an action research project based on an agreed focus by staff participating in the project. If needed, begin with only one department that is interested in the project.
- Make sure participants understand the project's focus before, during, and after the project.
- Action research should not be too demanding on the teachers' time.

- Develop a timeline to gather student work samples, to examine the data and reflect on the trends and insights across the evidence.
- Schedule dedicated time on the school calendar for faculty work sessions (45- to 75-minute sessions). Use department meetings or alternative scheduling options for instructional minutes in your district or county (see Chapter 4, Professional Development).
- Review prior student performance data with your staff. Let your staff be part of the discussion as to what the data are "saying" about student performance. Listen to their questions and assumptions as the staff interprets the data. If you need additional information, consult someone who is an expert in data analysis.
- Some staff may benefit from other professional development opportunities such as: developing rubrics, curriculum mapping, and analyzing student performance data.
- Include staff and student voices on the planning team.
- Report to stakeholders what you have learned as a result of the project.
- Think about the next steps. Put results into action after the project has concluded. How will the findings support improving student achievement?
- Shared decision making is vital in the area of action research.
- Be clear about the purpose of an action research project. Action research can provide data to inform curriculum and instruction; identify staff development needs; and provide a structure to pause and reflect upon the effects of teaching and learning.
- Provide time within the structure of the work year for teachers to plan, implement, reflect upon, and modify action research.
- Planning time is necessary for department staff to review the topics covered on the high-stakes tests. Have each department prepare a sequence of study for each semester that all department staff will follow. Be sure the sequence of study aligns to high-stakes testing dates. Determine the dates throughout the year when the department staff will review student work from predetermined lessons or units of study.
- Provide information and professional development opportunities for staff to become familiar with and practice using rubrics to assess student performance.

BKHS Case Study 2: Connecting Action Research to District Mandates

Birch Knoll High School

Principal Carl A. just completed the required principal workshop on action research. Carl shared the superintendent's enthusiasm and saw how this type of project could help reduced the number of D and F grades on his campus. He believed that if teachers would just teach what was tested, then student performance scores would improve and everyone would be happy. The action research project appeared simple: collect samples of student work three times during the school year; have a group of faculty review the samples to identify which teachers were not teaching the curriculum; and then meet with those teachers and give them examples of how other staff were able to get the job done.

Carl was excited about telling his co-administrators about the new project. The next day, Carl met with his administrative staff and explained how the action research project would work. He told one of his co-administrators to prepare an administrative bulletin describing the project. This bulletin would be shared with the faculty at the next staff meeting in two days. Carl was pleased with his plan.

At the beginning of the second semester, Carl requested that each department chair submit a report of the progress of the action research project. He was disappointed in the responses he received. It seemed that only the math department had collected student work samples during the first semester. According to Carl's co-administrators, the other departments had not participated in the action research project for a variety of reasons: changing teacher assignments during the first two weeks of school, implementation of the student portfolio requirements that had taken priority, general apathy, and lack of follow-through.

The report from the math department chair indicated that the teachers agreed to review the first set of student work collected in September. The department did not meet again until December due to textbook selection meetings, and therefore did not review the September student work samples until that time. In the report, the math teachers indicated that it appeared that most students did not have a grasp of basic number sense. The department chair reported that the department determined this data was insightful and that teachers would focus on number sense the following year.

Carl summarized the report from the math department and submitted the information to the superintendent.

Points to Consider

- An action research project must have a purpose and focus.
- Action research requires pre-planning.
- Action research requires staff buy-in.
- Action research will not "fix" anyone.
- Action research is only one piece of assessment data to consider when a Single School Plan is developed to improve student performance.
- Be prepared for some teachers to be uncomfortable working with peers. Provide opportunities for staff to get to know each other and learn from each other.
- Do not violate your teachers' contract.

Summary

Involving staff in meaningful projects is one of the hurdles site administrators face when managing complex change in secondary schools. Many staff members immediately want to "see results" of their efforts to meet the demands for improving student performance. Using action research as one of the components of a school's strategic action plan provides site administrators with an opportunity for all stakeholders to become active partners in the efforts to improve student performance. Action research allows teachers to collaborate with colleagues and become active participants in a project that gathers data, reflects on trends and insights, and applies new learning strategies based upon research results within the same school year.

In this chapter, we examined how two site administrators approached the concept of using action research to gather information about the effect of instructional strategies on student learning. Their purposes varied from compliance with a new district mandate to using action research as a vehicle for analyzing data to inform teaching and learning. Each site administrator "implemented" an action research project. Both site administrators received feedback on the implementation process.

The first steps to implementing an action research project are to identify a valid need for the project, then provide opportunities for staff members to become competent in conducting a successful action research project. Sample agendas for faculty meetings have been included at the end of this chapter for site administrators to use to prepare staff to discover the benefits of an action research project. Points to consider are presented for the reader's reflection.

It is important to have a purpose for the activity, a plan for implementation, and a willingness to support the staff to plan, teach, reflect, and apply the lessons from student work.

Application Activity

Before your team meets for the first time, take time to reflect on the following questions:

Who should be invited to participate on the Action Research Project Team?

What data is currently collected that addresses common indicators of a successful school?

What are my responsibilities for the success of this project?

What resources are needed from district office personnel to successfully implement this project?

What protocols will be used during action research conversations?

By what date do I need the action research data in order to prepare a summative report on this project?

What are some strategies that can be used to provide time, within the structure of the work year, for teachers to plan, implement, reflect upon, and modify action research?

What are the indicators of a successful school?

Ask each stakeholder group to identify what it believes are indicators of a successful school. The following simple chart provides space for each group to list indicators. Next, identify common indicators for all groups. These common indicators will provide you with a better focus for your action research.

Stakeholder Group	*Indicators of a Successful School*
Community	
Institute of Higher Education (IHE)	
District Governing Board	
Parents	
Students	
Staff	

Sample Agendas for Staff Meetings

The following sample agendas provide models for initiating action research.

Staff Work Session Agenda (1)

Objective: Understand how action research informs teaching and learning. Assess the need for action research.

After the staff has viewed a short video about action research, conduct a discussion on how action research might be carried out at your school.

Discussion Prompts:

- What is action research?
- How does it inform teaching and learning?
- How might action research assist our school to improve student performance?
- What roadblocks might there be if our school wants to use action research to assess student learning?
- What will be our next step?

Staff Work Session Agenda (2)

Objective: Curriculum alignment. Create an action plan.

- Review the purpose of action research.
- *Whole group:* Review alignment between content standards and sample test questions contained in annual student performance assessments.
- *Small group:* Align district curriculum goals and objectives to the content areas in annual student performance assessments.

Materials needed:

1. Guidebook and/or test samples for annual student performance assessments

2. State and district curriculum standards

3. Course descriptions

4. District testing calendar

Staff Work Session Agendas (3) and (4)

Objective: Compare and contrast student work samples covering a common assignment, with one set of examples coming from Explicit Direct Instruction lessons and another from lessons incorporating other instructional strategies (non-direct instruction).

Discussion Prompts:

- Does the lesson have an objective?
- Do student work samples reflect the lesson objective?
- Does student work sample meet the criteria for the lesson objective (rubric)?

    Separate student work into three categories—above standards, at standards, below standards for this lesson—based upon a common rubric agreed to by staff.

    Identify areas for reteaching (below standard).

    Identify areas for reinforcing learning (all levels).

    Identify areas for accelerated learning (above standard).

8

Productive Classroom Observations

Observe Often and With Purpose

Your superintendent has decided to visit your school and tour the classrooms. Do you know what is taking place in your classrooms? The prospect of "touring the classrooms" with the superintendent is perceived by some school leaders as an opportunity to highlight programs and lobby for more resources. Be prepared; these "tours" are becoming a popular activity in many districts.

Secondary school leaders engaged in educational reform efforts must monitor not only what is occurring in the school but also what is happening in the classroom. Observation-by-proxy or evaluation-by-rumor is no longer sufficient for schools to meet federal and state accountability standards. Moreover, meeting accountability standards should not be the reason why classroom visitations take place. School leaders must understand how to gather and assess current, credible, factual, firsthand data about what is occurring in the classroom in order to provide meaningful dialogue with staff about best practices.

Beginning and experienced educators enter secondary school leadership positions at various stages of readiness to effectively assess the performance of teachers and/or to hold post-observation conferences. There are many purposes for classroom observations. This chapter will highlight three of them:

1. The formal teacher performance evaluation (some employee contract language uses the term "appraisal" instead of "evaluation")

2. Instructional accountability

3. Professional growth support

Purposes of Classroom Observations

Formal Teacher Performance Evaluation

A teacher performance evaluation is a formal and formative assessment process that results in a summative report outlining the objectives, performance data, and the supervisor's conclusion. The National Teaching Standards have established the foundation for teacher performance assessment and professional growth. Whether they address academic content or performance, standards provide specific criteria upon which teachers (and students) are assessed. Teaching standards identify what teachers should know and be able to do, relative to classroom instruction. Classroom observations are essential for gathering evidence for this type of assessment.

Instructional Accountability

Recent educational reform efforts require that teachers demonstrate the ability to provide effective classroom instruction that is aligned with current national and/or state academic content standards. The *No Child Left Behind Act* of 2001 clearly delineates how teachers can meet the academic content knowledge criteria that every teacher serving in a Title I school or district must demonstrate. District office administrators generally provide guidance for teachers in how to meet this requirement. The second component of instructional accountability is the assessment of classroom instruction. At the school site, classroom teacher observation is one effective technique many secondary school leaders use to record teacher performance, discover instructional trends, and identify topics for professional growth.

Professional Growth Support

Greater numbers of secondary school leaders are participating in professional development opportunities to keep current on the latest teacher support, curricular and instructional practices, and assessment research. Coaching and support systems have been developed by states and districts for school leaders to use in the classrooms. Teacher training and retention are goals of many district-level coaching and support programs. Teacher retention data is commonly required in many educational reform efforts.

Professional development activities sponsored by schools, districts, and/or county offices of education are designed to provide teachers opportunities to learn more about research-based strategies to improve student achievement and how to align curriculum, instruction, and assessment (see Chapter 4, Professional Development). Traditionally, these professional development opportunities are offered to educators prior to the beginning of the school year. Paradoxically, a good number of secondary school leaders are obliged to wait to hire a percentage of teachers until after the school year begins, when student enrollment can be verified. This hiring delay precludes many teachers from attending the most beneficial professional development due to the uncertainty of the teaching assignment. Nevertheless, secondary school leaders are compelled to guarantee that all classroom teachers understand and use effective research-based instructional strategies to improve student achievement. Observing teaching and learning in the classroom and participating in reflective dialogue (Downey et al., 2004) with teachers are strategies successful school leaders use to support professional growth and improve student achievement.

Formal and Informal Classroom Observations

Productive classroom observations take place when there is a mutual agreement between the observer and the teacher about their purpose. Formal observations frequently refer to those observations required under employee contract for a formative and/or summative performance evaluation. Formal classroom observations are a key accountability activity for school leaders. For the purpose of this chapter, informal observations include observations for instructional monitoring and professional growth.

Similarities

- Classroom observations are essential for gathering evidence for both the formal (evaluation) and informal (strengthen instruction and curriculum alignment) teacher assessments.

- Both types of observations gather information based on specific *evidence, not opinion.*
- Both observations look for alignment between curriculum and instruction (Downey et al., 2004).

  Curriculum is non-negotiable. It is composed of the approved state standards and/or district course descriptions. Instructional objectives should clearly align with state standards or curriculum guides.

  Instruction refers to the way the teacher teaches the curriculum. It includes teaching practices, student groupings, how students are taught the information in the standards, how the text and supplemental learning materials are used, questioning strategies, checking for understanding, formative assessment, and so forth.

Differences

- Elements of a *formal* classroom observation are usually outlined in the employee contract.
- Employee contracts may also include a collaborative self-assessment process as an alternative evaluation of teacher performance. This option is usually available for veteran teachers with an outstanding record of prior classroom performance. The teacher generally requests this option with approval by the principal. Many teachers participating in the National Board Certification process elect this option.
- *Informal* classroom observations to strengthen instruction and curriculum alignment are strategic. In many districts, this type of observation is referred to as a "classroom walk-through" (Downey & Palo Verde Associates, 1999). These observations are frequent, brief (3 to 10 minutes), and focus on four key elements: (1) time on task, (2) curriculum content (the objective of the instruction), (3) context—conditions for learning aligned to content (student orientation to work and instructional decisions in the classroom), and (4) cognitive level of learning activity.
- *Informal* classroom observations to support professional growth are usually more like coaching in nature. Peer coaches, staff developers, and site administrators often conduct these types of observations.

In short, the formal classroom observation for teacher evaluation is contractual. The rewards and consequences of a performance evaluation are employment related. Classroom observations to strengthen instruction and curriculum alignment are usually informal, frequent, and brief. The eventual result of both the formal and informal processes is the improvement of student achievement.

Getting Started

Assess the Need

Schools involved in critical reforms or legislative mandates must verify the completion of all three types of classroom observations: (1) performance evaluation, (2) instructional accountability, and (3) professional growth support.

If a school is engaged in a reform or a legislative mandate process, it is always important to prioritize classroom observations based on the goals for the year. This is especially important for schools identified as "Program Improvement" under the guidelines established by the *No Child Left Behind Act* of 2001.

School leaders can identify which teachers are scheduled for performance evaluations based on employee contract language. Using student performance data, leaders can identify which department(s) will need support for curricular and instructional accountability as well as professional development.

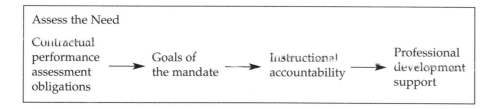

Create a Plan

Implementing classroom observations requires a strategy to prioritize goals, organize visits, and follow through with reflective conversations. At the opening-of-school meetings, communicate a workable, realistic plan for conducting classroom observations and identify their purposes. Communicate how the observer will be collecting data during the classroom observation. Collecting data during any type of classroom observation must be based on observable evidence, not opinion.

During individual teacher conferences, it is an effective practice to review the purpose for a specific classroom observation prior to each visit. "Pop quizzes" are stressful for students; "pop-in teacher observations" are stressful for both students and the teacher, and they usually do not help build trust between the teacher and administrator. However, with proper preparation and orientation, both students and staff will become more comfortable with people "popping by" the classrooms to support curricular and instructional decisions and professional growth.

Gather Data

How much time does it take to conduct effective classroom observations, and how often should they be done? To answer this, first identify the purpose for the classroom observation.

- Are you observing to evaluate the teacher?
   Formal, contractual, requires multiple observations, generally for a full class period.
- Are you observing to strengthen instruction and curriculum alignment?
   Informal, usually non-contractual, requires multiple observations, but much shorter in length.
- Are you observing for professional support or development?
   Informal, usually non-contractual, requires multiple observations, and may require a full class period or a shorter "snapshot."

Observational Tools

Many districts and/or administrators use a simple checklist to conduct classroom observations. This checklist might be through the lens of the National Teaching Standards or it might reflect the elements of a lesson. Some follow the Clinical Supervision model of scripting lessons. Others believe that a checklist is not necessary because the observer is looking for curricular and instructional decisions for professional reflective dialogue (Downey et al., 2004). Regardless of the observational process used, the purpose is to collect specific, observable data to be used in assessing classroom practice and student learning.

A sample checklist (Figure 8.1) developed by Sylvia Ibarra and John Hollingsworth (2002) is based on the direct instruction model and outlines specific elements they feel should be included in every EDI (Explicit Direct Instruction) lesson. It is the opinion of the authors that many of these elements (noted with an asterisk) should be incorporated into *every* lesson, regardless of the instructional model. As noted on the checklist, teachers should be overtly checking for every student's understanding throughout the lesson. This is not done by simply asking, "Are there any questions?"

Figure 8.1   Explicit Direct Instruction Final Checklist

Component	Checklist	Yes	No	Don't Know
*Learning Objectives— Independent Work	1. Does the Learning Objective match the content standards? 2. Does the Learning Objective have a situation (context)? 3. Does the Learning Objective have a measurable behavior? 4. Does the independent work match the Learning Objective?			
*Check for Understanding	5. Does the lesson allow for cyclical checking for understanding? (Think, Pair, Share; Finger Signals; whiteboards, etc.)			
*Preview	6. Is activating prior knowledge connected to information students are familiar with?			
*Review	7. Is activating prior knowledge connected to content the students have been taught before?			
Check for Understanding	8. Does the lesson allow for cyclical checking for understanding?			
*Explain	9. Does the lesson explain what it is? 10. Does the lesson explain how it is done? 11. Does the lesson explain why it is important?			
Check for Understanding	12. Does the lesson allow for cyclical checking for understanding?			
Model	13. Are the teacher's inner thoughts included during modeling? (Thinking the process through out loud)			
Check for Understanding	14. Does the lesson allow for cyclical checking for understanding?			
Demonstrate	15. Does the lesson show a way of demonstrating how to do something?			
Check for Understanding	16. Does the lesson allow for cyclical checking for understanding?			
*Guided Practice	17. Is a process being taught? 18. Are facts being taught? 19. Is the guided practice providing sufficient practice on all the material that the students will be asked to complete independently? 20. Does the lesson include lots of questions?			
Check for Understanding	21. Does the lesson allow for cyclical checking for understanding?			
*Closure	22. Does the lesson provide opportunities for all students to show what they have learned?			

(Continued)

Figure 8.1   (Continued)

Component	Checklist	Yes	No	Don't Know
Check for Understanding	23. Does the lesson allow for cyclical checking for understanding?			
*Independent Practice	24. Have all the skills needed for the independent practice been taught so students can do independent practice successfully?			
*Daily Success	25. Is homework in sync with the Learning Objective?			
Periodic Review	26. Do students have opportunities to revisit the same concepts?			
*Mastery	27. Are quizzes and tests in sync with what students have been taught?			

Adapted from *The Target Improvement Model* (2002), copyrighted materials by Ibarra, S., and Hollingsworth, J. Fowler, CA: DataWorks Educational Research.

Making Time for Observations

Due to the large size of a secondary school staff, many school leaders look for ways to effectively schedule teacher observation for performance evaluation as well as to observe teachers for professional support and growth. It's very easy to lose track of time as the year progresses and get behind. The following is a suggested protocol for organizing observations:

- Get a calendar of the school year and cross out the holidays, mark the end of every grading period, and make your best guess for assembly dates. Next, block out finals week plus the week prior, list district meetings you must attend, highlight contractual deadlines, and eliminate the Fridays and Mondays attached to holidays.
- Count the remaining number of days (typically around 85 to 90 days).
- Take the number of teachers scheduled for performance evaluations this year, multiply by the contractual number of minutes (or class periods) you must observe a teacher, add 1 extra class period per teacher (something always happens), and set aside that number of class periods for contractual classroom observations. Example: 27 teachers to observe times 2 contractual observation periods per teacher plus 27 extra periods equals 81 class periods of observation time needed on your schedule. That is nearly 14 full days just to meet contractual obligations! Realistically,

principals block out 2 to 3 periods for observations at a time. Now you need to block out time over at least 27 days!

- Plan time for classroom observations to strengthen instruction and support professional growth. Count the number of teachers in each of the departments you want to focus on this year. Multiply the number of identified teachers times 20 minutes. That number represents how much time you will need to set aside from your schedule to visit those teachers 5 times during the school year. Example: There are 15 teachers you would like to visit to strengthen instruction and support professional growth, multiplied by 20 minutes per teacher equals 300 minutes. By conducting short, focused classroom observations, you can support professional growth for nearly a quarter of your staff using only 5 hours of your time in the classroom!

Reflection/Post-Conferences

Schedule time to reflect and debrief with teachers as soon as possible after the observation. These conferences may be formal conversations documenting the completion of mutually agreed-upon instructional goals and objectives developed by the teacher. Or, post-observation conferences may be reflective conversations geared to providing informal feedback about brief classroom observations.

More than ever before, secondary school leaders are asked to be multitasking, problem-solving change agents. Keeping some form of organizational system is vital. Whether this system is organized by projects or the time of the year, effective school leaders rely on these systems for future planning.

Revise or Modify Tools

Tools include the observation calendar and note-taking worksheets. Until a school leader is proficient in recognizing the currently approved content and performance standards in action, it is helpful to utilize note-taking worksheets or checklists for classroom observations and progress monitoring (see Figure 8.1). Always provide teachers with a copy of the template before classroom observations take place.

Case Studies

The following case studies illustrate two different approaches for organizing and implementing classroom observations. The first case study reveals a purposeful, organized plan to incorporate classroom observations into the professional development plan as well as the evaluation process. The second case study identifies how classroom observations are commonly used to fulfill contract obligations.

RVMS   Case Study 1: Learning and Supervising With Observation

Ridge View Middle School

Principal Tony R. has completed his second year at Ridge View Middle School. He has two co-administrators to assist him with the 25 teacher-performance evaluations this year. Tony would like to support the teachers participating in this year's action research project (see Chapter 7) by walking through classrooms and becoming familiar with the instructional activities taking place.

Tony met with his two co-administrators at the end of the previous year to identify the staff members scheduled for a formal performance evaluation for the upcoming school year. Next, his team listed the teachers leading and participating in the action research project. Tony's team divided up the 25 evaluation assignments in a way that attempted to prevent an administrator from conducting a formal evaluation with the same teacher that administrator was assigned to support for professional growth. This task proved difficult because there were a number of teachers who fell into both categories. Nevertheless, the team was satisfied with its decision. Tony would be evaluating the 10 first- and second-year teachers along with three teachers currently on a directed assistance plan. Each of the co-administrators would be responsible for the evaluation of six veteran teachers plus half of the 12 classified staff members.

At the preservice meeting, Tony presented the faculty with information about performance evaluations and professional development support. He reviewed the purposes for the three different types of classroom observations he and his co-administrators hoped to conduct throughout the year: (1) performance evaluation, (2) instructional accountability, and (3) professional development support.

Tony distributed the list of teachers scheduled for performance evaluation during the current year. He also gave those teachers a copy of the school calendar, the employee contract section addressing performance evaluation, and copies of the progress-monitoring and note-taking worksheets he and his co-administrators were going to use during the classroom observations.

Next, Tony led a discussion about the importance of aligning instruction and student assessment with state content standards. He and the department chairpersons reviewed the key concepts of the curriculum alignment workshop the faculty had participated in during the previous year. He stated an expectation that every teacher would post the state content standard and related behavioral objective for each day's lesson.

Tony outlined the informal classroom observation procedures he and his co-administrators would be using to support the efforts of the action research project. Either Tony or one of his co-administrators would become a member of the learning team during the action research project. He invited teachers to stop by the office after school to discuss any of the visits.

Finally, Tony shared the different worksheets he and his co-administrators would be using this year. He invited the staff to provide suggestions for improvement on the feedback forms at any time.

Figure 8.2 Sample Progress-Monitoring Worksheet

Progress-Monitoring Worksheet—Formal Evaluation (school year) Contractual deadlines (CD) and actual dates (AD) of conferences and classroom observations listed below.								
	Goals & Objectives	1st pre-observation meeting	1st observation	1st post-observation conference	2nd pre-observation meeting	2nd observation	2nd post-observation conference	Formal review of findings
Name of Teacher	CD= AD=	CD= AD=	CD= AD=	CD= AD=	CD= AD=	CD= AD=	CD= AD=	CD= AD=

Figure 8.3   Sample Classroom Note-Taking Worksheet for Observation

Date: _____	Teacher: _____	Class: _____
Observer (please print): _____ Start/Stop Times _____		

CLASSROOM OBSERVATION

Mutually agreed-upon goals and objectives	Observed	Observed evidence	Curriculum & Instruction Guide*
(List goal here)	☐		**Time on Task**
Objective 1	☐		**Content** (curriculum objectives, observed or listed, aligned with district curriculum)
Objective 2	☐		
	☐		**Context** (conditions for learning, alignment with content)
	☐		Student Activity
Teaching Standard			Teacher Activity
1	☐		Student work displayed
2	☐		
3	☐		Safety issues
4	☐		Cognitive level of learning activity (Bloom's Taxonomy)
5	☐		☐ Knowledge

Type of Evidence:

☐ Observed behavior
☐ Numeric information
☐ Aspect of the environment
☐ Dialogue used by teacher or student

Post-observation conference date:

Cognitive level of learning activity (Bloom's Taxonomy)

☐ Knowledge
☐ Comprehension
☐ Application
☐ Analysis
☐ Synthesis
☐ Evaluation

*Adapted from Carolyn Downey Walk-Thru workshop. Loren Tarantino, 2000.

At the end of three months, Tony and his co-administrators compiled all of the evidence collected during classroom observations. Based on the evidence, they quickly noticed three emerging trends:

1. Observed student-learning activities focused mainly on "knowledge" and "comprehension" skills.

2. In 90 percent of the lessons observed, teachers were not actively engaging students or checking for understanding.

3. Teachers working in the 200 building were unable to maximize the classroom space for student learning due to the location of the whiteboards and storage cabinets.

Tony met with the faculty advisory committee to present these findings. The committee recommended that a team of teachers and administrators identify specific professional development activities to offer staff during the professional development days in March and June. The focus for the professional development would be increasing critical-thinking activities and strategies for actively engaging students in the learning process.

Tony met with the teachers in the 200 building and requested suggestions for ways to improve the learning environment in their classrooms. On the basis of those suggestions, Tony contacted the district's facilities department manager and submitted a work order to change the location of the whiteboards in several of the classrooms.

Points to Consider

- Effective school leaders are learners. National and local educational organizations and consultants are available to provide professional development for teachers and administrators in the areas of standards alignment, classroom observations, and coaching skills.
- Submit a draft copy of all note-taking guides and worksheets you plan to use in the informal observation process to the appropriate district administrator prior to distribution to the faculty. Formal observation documents generally are part of the bargaining unit contract.
- It is better to ask for permission than to ask for forgiveness when it comes to contractual procedures. For example, do not alter the district evaluation form or change the evaluation timeline unless you first obtain permission from the HR office.

- Be visible outside the main office.
- Practice observation and coaching skills with a co-administrator.
- Take time at the end of the school year to identify staff members scheduled for the evaluation process the following year. Involve co-administrators during the planning process.
- Review student-performance assessment data to determine what content area support or instructional accountability observations might be needed for the following year. For example, many schools focus on math, literacy, and direct instruction of the state content standards.
- School leaders new to a school or district can receive information about staff evaluation policies and personnel concerns from co-administrators and human resources personnel at the district.
- Keep a copy of the evaluation information packet submitted to faculty during preservice meetings in a tickler file for the second month of school as a reminder to check to be sure teachers and administrators have met to discuss the evaluation process.

Case Study 2: Connecting Classroom Observations to Contract Obligations

Birch Knoll High School

As a first-year principal, Carl A. was a bit overwhelmed by the timeline he was required to follow in order to complete the 57 teacher-performance evaluations for the year. Compounding this problem, Carl received a letter from the district office notifying him that as a Program Improvement school (NCLB), Birch Knoll High School was scheduled for a visit by a state team in February. The letter indicated that the school needed to provide the state team with evidence documenting the progress the school was making to improve student achievement as identified in the benchmarks established over the past three quarters. Carl was hoping his new secretary would remember where those progress reports were filed. The district superintendent had required all school principals to attend an efficiency training session last year and there were no file cabinets in his new office, so he had no idea where to look for materials from that training.

Carl met with his co-administrators prior to the first week of school to discuss the teacher-evaluation schedule. Carl explained that the three co-administrators would each be assigned 16 teachers to evaluate. Carl would evaluate the remaining nine teachers plus prepare for the state team visit.

Carl delegated the responsibility of notifying the faculty about the evaluation process to one of his co-administrators. He provided time at the next faculty meeting for his co-administrator to review the evaluation process and contractual obligations. A copy of the teacher-performance evaluation section of the employee contract was distributed with a list of teachers scheduled to participate in the evaluation process.

Carl noticed that his co-administrator had designed his own observation worksheet. He hoped that it did not contain anything that might lead to a grievance by the teachers' association.

Next, Carl shared information about the "Program Improvement, Year 3" status of the school and the district's expectations to demonstrate improved student performance in the areas of language arts and mathematics before the upcoming state visit in February. He distributed a copy of the letter he had received from the district office outlining the consequences for staff and students if the student performance goals were not achieved by the end of the school year. Carl noticed that many of the 100 teachers at the meeting left somewhat dazed when they realized how serious the problems were at Birch Knoll High School. It was evident that most of the staff had had no idea how the student performance data could impact everyone in the school.

Over the next three months, Carl and his co-administrators met with the teachers scheduled for performance evaluations to complete the required forms. Administrators visited each teacher's classroom once. Post-observation conferences were held within four weeks of the classroom observation.

Carl made several attempts to wander through the halls and peer into the classrooms; however, he soon became bogged down with the logistics of preparing for the state team's visit and rarely left his office. By the end of November, Carl was feeling isolated and out of touch with the students and teachers due to the lack of time spent outside his office. He had not completed his second round of classroom observations and the superintendent was requesting an update on the evaluation process from every principal.

At the end of the first semester, Carl was exhausted. He and his co-administrators had prepared the report for the superintendent, outlining the procedure they were using to complete the evaluation process. Although Carl had met the contractual obligations for teacher evaluations, he realized he really did not know what was going on in the classrooms. Carl made a pledge to himself that he would get out of his office just as soon as the state visit was completed.

Points to Consider

- Time is a resource. Budget time for classroom observations. Make this time a high priority. This is easier said than done. Particularly if you are a new principal, be sure to set realistic goals.
- Delegation of major responsibilities can work, as long as the principal communicates the importance of the task. Delegate; don't abdicate or isolate.
- Scheduling weekly meetings to discuss school logistics with co-administrators leads to opportunities for problem solving and staying connected.
- Block out enough time (2 to 3 hours) to thoroughly discuss school issues and provide updates to co-administrators from the district office.

Summary

Satisfying the contractual teacher-performance evaluation process is the most common reason that teachers have been observed in the past. Strengthening the alignment between curriculum, instruction, and assessment and giving support for professional growth are additional reasons secondary school leaders conduct classroom observations. Assessing teacher performance and instructional accountability have become essential tasks for today's instructional leader.

In this chapter, we took a look at how two site administrators approached the concept of using classroom observations to improve student achievement. Their purposes varied from compliance with district, state, and/or federal mandates to using classroom observations as a vehicle for managing some of the complexities of using data to inform teaching and learning. Although each site administrator from the case studies "implemented" classroom observations, they each had very different levels of success based on actual participation in the process.

Application Activity

Activity: Classroom Observation Data Collection

Understanding the difference between "evidence" and "opinion" is one of the basic skills needed for conducting effective classroom observations. Feedback is important for improving instruction. When the observer is skilled in collecting data, it improves the conversations between the observer and the person being observed.

Research in teacher induction programs has provided teachers and administrators with a practical guide for distinguishing between evidence and opinion (California Beginning Teacher Support and Assessment, 2003).

1. Review the following definitions of "evidence" and "opinion." Ask the group for classroom examples of each statement.

Evidence

- Is observable (you can see it or hear it)
- Is not influenced by observer's perspective
- Is free of evaluative words
- Is non-conclusive

Opinion

- Makes assumptions
- Depends on observer's perspective
- Includes evaluative words (e.g., good, okay, great job, disturbing)
- Draws conclusions

2. Review the types of evidence collected during classroom observations:
    - Numeric information (e.g., the amount of time spent during part of the lesson, the number of students participating in an activity, the number of times a teacher calls on students, the number of times and where a teacher moves)
    - Writing exactly what the teacher or student says
    - Observed behavior (teacher or student)
    - An observed aspect of the environment

3. Following this review, show a video of an actual classroom instruction. (Check with the district offices to see what they have available.)

- Each participant "observes" and collects evidence from the video lesson.
- Carousel Activity: Using national or state standards for the teaching profession, make a chart for each element of one teaching standard. Post around the room. Participants number off by the number of charts and carousel at 2- to 3-minute intervals. Task: write on the chart as many examples of evidence for the given element as possible before the signal to move on to the next chart.
- In pairs or table groups, participants report on data collected. A determination is made on whether the data constitutes evidence or opinion.

9

Putting the Pieces Together

Secondary schools, by their very nature, are incredibly complex and fluid organizations. Leadership challenges include management and supervision of athletics, student activities, certificated and classified staff, school safety, facilities, professional development, and instructional programs to meet the needs of all students (building a Master Schedule that reflects adequate intervention and support classes). To add to the challenge, more often than not, secondary schools are much larger than elementary schools, with 1,000 to 4,000 students.

With the implementation of the *No Child Left Behind Act* of 2001 and the subsequent accountability measures undertaken by states throughout the nation, there is tremendous pressure on school administrators and teachers to specifically address the requirements of the law and to ensure that every child is provided with a strong, standards-based curriculum taught by Highly Qualified Teachers, as well as provide specific interventions designed to remediate the individual knowledge and skill deficiencies of students in math and language arts. This book has focused on the challenges associated with moving secondary schools through the design and implementation of a school reform process, on research that outlines strategies that work, and on opportunities for readers to apply new information to their own school organization.

The following Sample Implementation Checklist provides a list of steps to be considered by school leaders in initiating and implementing reform efforts.

Sample Implementation Checklist for Secondary School Leaders

1. Identify specific tasks that need to be accomplished throughout the year. Then analyze tasks to determine where, if applicable, tasks might be combined.

   This can be done with input from your secretary, the guidance department chairperson, and teacher leaders.

2. Set up a timeline on the calendar for task deadlines (carved in stone).

   It is important to do this. If not, things will slip through the cracks.

3. Identify the most current mandates, grant requirements, district priorities, and reforms that impact the school.

   Be very clear about the district and state mandates related to standards-based curriculum, instructional materials, assessment systems and requirements, teacher credentialing (Highly Qualified Teacher issues), and professional development. In addition, connections should be made with any school or district grants or reform initiatives already in place.

4. Gather and review all pertinent documents.

   These may include, but are not limited to, items such as the accreditation report, disaggregated student assessment data, school accountability report cards to the community, school discipline and safety data, bargaining unit contracts, technology plan, staff development plan, Title I plan, school policies and handbooks, athletic guidelines, Master Schedule, bell schedule, courses of study, graduation requirements, textbook inventory, science inventory, school newspaper, and so forth. This will assist you in determining "how we do business around here" (Chapter 1). It will also assist you in the development of a Single School Plan (Chapter 3). Compile all documents into one binder or file drawer for easy access throughout the year.

5. Clearly communicate to staff the mandates for reform and the tasks that need to be accomplished, as well as opportunities to actively participate in the process.

    Continue to keep staff informed throughout the year at staff meetings, through regular e-mail updates, and through newsletters. Add a staff communication timeline to the implementation calendar.

6. Identify key stakeholders to participate in the planning process.

    Identifying key stakeholders doesn't necessarily require that the principal, if new to the school, know who the key players are among teachers, classified staff, parents, community, and students. However, it *is* necessary to know where to go to get that information if you are new to the site and/or the community. Check committee rosters to identify the parents, staff, and students who are already participating in the decision-making process. Identify the "priests and priestesses," and other staff members who might assist or impede the change process. Talk to the school secretary, your co-administrators, the head counselor, and the lead custodian (see Chapter 1)!

7. Assemble the School Site Council.

    Determine a meeting calendar for the year. Review the current district and school vision and mission statements, and update the school vision and mission, as needed.

8. With the School Site Council, systematically review the student assessment data.

    Data should be disaggregated by gender, race, ethnicity, language proficiency, special needs, socioeconomic status, and grade level. Whenever possible, longitudinal data should be made available to demonstrate the academic progress of students as they progress through each grade within the school. Identify areas of strength and areas of need relative to achievement of grade-level standards by all subgroups (see Chapter 3).

    a. What student subgroups are not meeting grade-level standards in mathematics and language arts (reading), based upon state and, if available, district benchmark data?

    b. What percentage/number of students is not meeting grade-level standards? This information will impact the Master Schedule as intervention classes are determined.

You will need to know who those students are, by name, for placement into intervention programs.

9. Based upon the vision of the school and the assessed areas of need to improve student achievement, begin the action planning process to create a Single School Plan.

   Add benchmark target dates to the implementation calendar (see Chapter 3).

   a. Identify specific intervention classes, programs, and instructional materials (must often be state-approved) to provide targeted and individualized support and intervention to students who have not met grade-level standards in mathematics and language arts (reading).
   b. Develop a system for identifying, scheduling into appropriate interventions, and ongoing monitoring of those students who have not met grade-level standards. This will impact the Guidance Department and core subject departments.
   c. Identify staff needs relative to research-based instructional strategies and the use of new instructional materials (see Chapter 4).

10. Assess the level of parent and community involvement. Develop and implement a plan to maximize communication with and support for parent involvement.

    After reading Chapter 6 and gathering data on the number and subgroups of parents who are involved in school activities and projects, identify some specific measure you will take to improve parent involvement in your school.

11. Develop a comprehensive system for communicating with parents, community, staff, and students (see Chapter 6).

    a. Develop a staff phone tree for emergency notifications (your secretary will do this).
    b. Utilize a school Web site, e-mail, parent/community newsletters, and so forth to communicate with parents and community.
    c. Participate as a member of a community organization such as Rotary International.
    d. Volunteer to do presentations about your school for local community organizations such as Rotary, Kiwanis, and local church groups.

12. Set up a tickler system (with your secretary) to monitor the implementation process and deadlines throughout the year.

13. Develop a comprehensive, differentiated professional development program.

    The professional development program should be aligned with the goals and objectives outlined in the Single School Plan. It should also offer differentiated training and support to staff according to the LOU (Levels of Use) stages and levels of knowledge and previous experience. One size does not fit all (see Chapter 4)!

14. Begin the development and implementation of a professional learning community at your school.

    Start with an overview of the concept of a professional learning community (Chapter 5). The key to making this happen is a vision and expectation by the school leadership that all staff participate in this model. Provide a structure and essential questions to guide the conversations during department meetings and those of other pertinent committees, such as the Action Research Project Team (Chapter 7). Require sign-in sheets and meeting minutes and/or a product of some type.

15. Set the stage at the beginning of the year for ongoing formal and informal classroom observations.

It is important to begin to set the stage at the beginning of the year for formal and informal classroom observations throughout the year. Determine what templates will be used, provide copies, and review with staff. (Check first to be sure there are no conflicts with bargaining unit agreements regarding the documents being used.) Mark your calendar for formal observations and follow-up conferences; then block specific time each week to conduct informal classroom observations. Have your secretary protect your estimated time in the classrooms (see Chapter 8)!

Summary

Effectively leading a school through a reform process requires commitment, dedication, and considerable stamina. It also requires that school leaders carefully consider the school culture and utilize change theory as a map to navigate through the process. School safety and discipline issues can easily usurp the majority of available time unless a clear plan exists to ensure the ongoing, persistent journey forward. This journey cannot be accomplished in isolation. It is critical to identify, develop, and empower other school leaders (administrators, teachers, and classified staff) to move the reform agenda forward through day-to-day activities, processes, and systems that support the belief that every single student can learn and grow.

Appendix: Related Web Sites

www.acsa.org (Association of California School Administrators)

www.ascd.org (Association for Supervision and Curriculum Development)

www.assessmentinst.com (Assessment Training Institute)

www.btsa.ca.gov (California Beginning Teacher Support and Assessment)

www.cde.ca.gov (California Department of Education)

www.childtrendsdatabank.org/indicators/39/ParentInvolvement

www.colonialcambridge.com (The Cambridge Group)

www.ctc.ca.gov (California Commission on Teacher Credentialing)

www.eagle.ca (information about Edwards Deming and Total Quality Management)

www.ed.gov/Family

www.ed.gov/policy (U.S. Department of Education)

www.education-world.com

www.fiu.edu (Florida International University)

www.hbdi.com (Ned Herrmann, Whole Brain Technology)

www.newhorizons.org (New Horizons for Learning)

www.nlm.nih.gov (National Library of Medicine's online collection of the writings of Paul MacLean, including information about the theory of the Triune Brain)

www.nwrel.org (Northwest Regional Laboratories)

www.pdintl.org (Phi Delta Kappa International)

www.projectappleseed.org

www.pta.org/ptawashington/issues/esea.asp

www.skyenet.net (a simplified Total Quality Management diagnostic model) www.themindworks.com (The MindWorks, Inc.)

www.uq.net.au/action_research/arhome.html ("Action Research Resources" contains links to resources such as conference abstracts, books, and e-mail lists of people that can be contacted who support action research)

References

Alexander, D. (2003). *Brain power workshop*. Columbus, OH: The MindWorks Inc.

Boyd, V. (1992). *School context: Bridge or barrier to change?* Austin, TX: Southwest Educational Development Laboratory.

Buzan, T. (1991). *Use both sides of your brain*. New York: Plume.

California Department of Education. (n.d.) *The framework for analysis of school culture*. California School Leadership Academy Culture Module.

California Department of Education (2003, March). *NCLB Teacher Requirements Resource Guide*. Sacramento, CA: California Department of Education, Professional Development and Curriculum Support Division. Available online at http://www.cde.ca.gov/nclb/sr/tq/ index.asp

California Beginning Teacher Support and Assessment. (2003, February). *What is evidence? Induction: roles and responsibilities of K–12 school organizations*. Available online at http://www.btsa.ca.gov/ba/profdev/ profdev.html).

California Department of Education. (n.d.). *California field guide for teachers' professional development: Designs for learning*. Santa Cruz, CA: ToucanEd.

California Department of Education. (2004, March). *NCLB teacher requirements resource guide*. Available online at www.cde.ca.gov/nclb/sr/tq/ index.asp

The Cambridge Group. (2003, June). *Strategic Planning Internal Facilitator Institute*. Montgomery, AL. Available online at www.colonialcambridge.com

Corey, S. (1953). *Action research to improve school practice*. New York: Teachers College, Columbia University.

Downey, C. J., & Palo Verde Associates. (1999). *Workshop material from Deep Curriculum Alignment for Higher Student Achievement*. San Diego, CA.

Downey, C. J., Steffy, B., English, F., Frase, L., & Poston, W. K. Jr. (2004). *The three-minute classroom walk-through: Changing school supervisory practice one teacher at a time*. Thousand Oaks, CA: Corwin.

DuFour, R. (2003, December 11–12). *Building a professional learning community*. Paper presented at the Building Learning Communities conference, Cerritos, CA.

DuFour, R., & Eaker, R. (1998). *Professional learning communities at work*. Bloomington, IN: National Educational Service.

Fitzpatrick, K. (1997). *School improvement: Focusing on student performance*. Schaumburg, IL: National Study of School Education.

Fullan, M. (1999). *Changing forces: The sequel.* Philadelphia: Falmer.

Fullan, M. (2001). *Leading in a culture of change.* San Francisco: Jossey-Bass.

Fullan, M. (2003). *The moral imperative of school leadership.* Thousand Oaks, CA: Corwin.

Fullan, M., & Hargreaves, A. (1991). *What's worth fighting for in your school?* Toronto: Ontario Public School Teachers' Federation.

Guskey, T. R. (2000). *Evaluating professional development.* Thousand Oaks, CA: Corwin.

Hall, G. E., & Hord, S. M. (2001). *Implementing change: Patterns, principles, and potholes.* Boston: Allyn & Bacon.

Henderson, A. T., & Berla, N. (1994). *A new generation of evidence: The family is critical to student achievement.* Washington, DC: Center for Law and Education.

Ibarra, S., & Hollingsworth, J. (2002). *The target improvement model.* Fowler, CA: DataWorks Educational Research.

Johnson, B. (1993). Office of Educational Research and Improvement (OERI) Web site. U.S. Department of Education.

Joyce, B., & Showers, B. (2000). *Student achievement through staff development* (3rd ed.). White Plains, NY: Longman.

LaBahn, J. (1995). Education and parental involvement in secondary schools: Problems, solutions, and effects. *Educational Psychology Interactive.* Valdosta, GA: Valdosta State University. Available online at http:/chiron.valdosta.edu/whuitt/files/parinvol.html

The Ned Herrmann Group. (1985). *Herrmann Brain Dominance Instrument survey and summary report.* Lake Lure, NC: Author.

Patterson, J. L., Purkey, S. C., & Parker, J. V. (1986). *Productive school systems for a nonrational world.* Alexandria, VA: Association for Supervision and Curriculum Development.

Richter, J. (2002). *Principal's guide to effective family involvement: Partnering for school success.* Gaithersburg, MD: Aspen.

Sagor, R. D. (2000). *Guiding school improvement with action research.* Alexandria, VA: Association for Supervision and Curriculum Development.

Senge, P., Cambron-McCabe, N., Lucas, T., Smith, B., Dutton, J., & Kleiner, A. (2000). *Schools that learn: A fifth discipline fieldbook for educators, parents, and everyone who cares about education.* New York: Doubleday.

Thacker, J. L., & McInerney, W. D. (1992, Fall). Changing academic culture to improve student achievement in the elementary schools. *ERS SPECTRUM 10*(4), 18–23.

Westbrook, J., & Spiser-Albert, V. (2002). *Creating the capacity for change.* Alexandria, VA: Association for Supervision and Curriculum Development.

Index

brain research and, 77, 80
communications and,
48, 85
data and, 32, 105, 108,
119, 128, 129, 134, 135
learning communities
and, 41, 43, 47, 50,
63, 64, 80, 85
observations and,
30, 54, 71, 117, 130
parents and, 92, 98
planning and, 28, 43,
63, 70, 74
pressure for improving,
19, 20, 128
professional
development
and, 60, 63, 65,
66, 67, 85
research and, 103, 117
school culture and, 4, 5, 8,
74, 85
single school plans and,
39, 40, 43, 47,
69, 81, 136
standardized tests and, 84
teamwork and, 83
values and, 83
vision and, 136
Student diversity, xiv, xv, 12,
16–18
Students:
accountability and, 54
attendance of, 89
communications and, 136
curriculum for, 118.
See also Curriculum.
learning experiences for,
79–80
new, 92
observations and, 119–120
planning and, 26, 108.
See also Planning.
support and, 136
Substitutes, 47, 62, 68, 70, 72
Support, 38
coaching and, 116–117
data and, 65. *See also*
Data.
leadership and, 30, 35,
37, 38, 60, 62, 90
learning communities
and, 85
mentors and, 6, 35, 68, 72
observations and, 116

ongoing, 37
parents and, 90
planning and, 35.
See also Planning.
stakeholders and, 30, 35,
37, 38, 60, 62, 90
students and, 136
Surveys., 30, 34, 65,
69, 72, 105

T
Tarantino, L. R., xvii,
xix, 126
Teachers:
accountability and, 130.
See also
Accountability.
action research and, 104
contracts and, 17, 54,
110, 116, 117,
118, 119
credentials for, 134
curriculum and, 118.
See also Curriculum.
data and, 82, 116,
117, 118, 130
development of, 20
hiring, 117
leadership and, 70
NCLB and, 46
observations and, 115,
116, 123
performance of, 116,
110, 130
resistant, 32
substitutes for, 47,
62, 68, 70, 72
training and, 85,
116–117, 127
workshops and, 63, 67
See also Staff;
Stakeholders
Teams:
action research project,
105, 106, 111, 137
cabals and, 7
single school plan and, 40
Templates, 48, 49, 64,
123, 137, 144
Test scores, 30, 92
Thacker, J. L., 3
Time lines, 22, 35, 41,
47–48, 70.53
Title I, xiv, 89, 134
NCLB and, 116

Total Quality
Management, 80
Traditions, 3
behavior and, 10
beliefs and, 6
organizations and, 77
values and, 6.
See also Values.
Training, 62
coaching skills and, 68,
71, 117
leadership and, 62
levels of use and, 35, 137
opportunities for, 90
parents and, 90, 91, 98
teachers and, 85,
116–117, 127

V
Values:
change and, 4, 22.
See also Change.
guarding, 7
shared vision of,
15, 54, 85
stakeholders and, 78
student achievements
and, 83
traditional, 6
Vision:
leadership and, 35,
40–41, 43, 74,
137–138
stakeholders and, 41
student achievements
and, 136
Vision statements:
facilitators for, 15
leadership and, 35,
40–41, 43, 44, 48, 74
planning and, 40–41
Volunteers, 87, 88, 90, 91,
93, 96, 136

W
Westbrook, J., 21
Whispers, 7, 16
Whites *See* Caucasians
Worksheets, 125, 126,
127, 129
Workshops:
effective, 74
failure of, 59, 60
professional development
and, 63, 66, 67, 68, 70

CORWIN
PRESS

The Corwin Press logo—a raven striding across an open book—represents the union of courage and learning. Corwin Press is committed to improving education for all learners by publishing books and other professional development resources for those serving the field of K–12 education. By providing practical, hands-on materials, Corwin Press continues to carry out the promise of its motto: **"Helping Educators Do Their Work Better."**